COVER
Detail from Camillo Golgi's 1885 *Sulla Fina
Anatomia degli Organi Centrali del Sistema Nervoso.*

ISSUE 3 / SPRING 2024

EDITOR
ZACHARY DAVIS

ASSOCIATE EDITORS
RACHEL JARDINE · RACHAEL JOHNSON · BENJAMIN PETERS

MANAGING EDITOR
LORI FORSYTH

SENIOR EDITORS
KRISTINE HAGLUND · TYLER JOHNSON · ANNA THURSTON

SUBMISSIONS MANAGER
GRACE CARTER

COPYEDITOR
MARK MELVILLE

ART EDITOR
ESTHER HI'ILANI CANDARI

POETRY EDITOR
KATHRYN KNIGHT SONNTAG

FICTION EDITOR
JEANINE BEE

DIRECTOR OF MUSIC
ANDREW MAXFIELD

CREATIVE DIRECTORS
NICHOLAS (COLE) MELANSON · DOUGLAS THOMAS

PRODUCTION ASSISTANT
SUMMER C. CHRISTIANSEN

CONTRIBUTING EDITORS
SHAYLA FRANDSEN · SHARLEE MULLINS GLENN · ALLISON POND · ISAAC RICHARDS · CANDICE WENDT
CHARLOTTE WILSON

DIGITAL EDITOR
KATIE LEWIS

SOCIAL MEDIA EDITOR
CECE PROFFIT

NEWS EDITOR
JAXON WASHBURN

DIGITAL CREATIVE DIRECTOR
LONDAN DUFFIN

ORATORY EDITOR
ISAAC RICHARDS

FILM EDITORS
BARRETT BURGIN · CELENE MITCHELL

SCIENCE EDITOR
MADDY PETERSON

AUDIENCE ENGAGEMENT
EMMA ST. CLAIR

INTERNS
JULIA MORGAN · SAM PETERSEN

EDITORIAL STAFF
KYLE BELANGER · GIDEON BURTON · ANGELA CLYDE-BARRIONUEVO · CAROLEE FAIRBANKS · NATALIE HAMMON
LORREN LEMMONS · MARTHA PETERSEN · SARAH SAFSTEN · TANNER SANDBERG · JEANNA MASON STAY
JOSH STEVENSON · ZACH STEVENSON · SUNNY STIMMLER · CLINT WILLIAMS

ADVISORY BOARD
MATT BOWMAN · RICHARD BUSHMAN · JENNIFER FREY · JAMES GOLDBERG · GEORGE HANDLEY · RANDALL PAUL
SHARRONA PEARL · JANA RIESS · CHARLES STANG · LAUREL THATCHER ULRICH · ROSALYNDE WELCH

wayfaremagazine.org FaithMatters

ISSUE 3 (SPRING 2024)
WAYFARE MAGAZINE IS PUBLISHED BY THE FAITH MATTERS FOUNDATION
FOR INQUIRIES, PLEASE CONTACT WAYFARE@FAITHMATTERS.ORG

Aaron Douglas

ESSAYS

POEMS

INTERVIEW

REVIEWS

STORY

EXHIBITS

HYMN

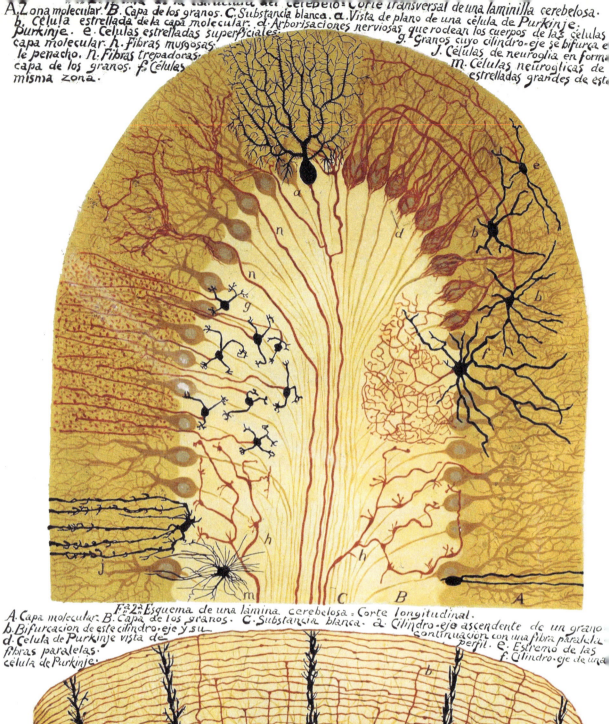

F.ª 2.ª Esquema de una lámina cerebelosa = Corte longitudinal.
A. Capa molecular. B. Capa de los granos. C. Substancia blanca. a. Cilindro-eje ascendente de un grano
b. Bifurcacion de este cilindro-eje y su continuacion con una fibra paralela.
d. Célula de Purkinje vista de perfil. e. Estremo de las
fibras paralelas. f. Cilindro-eje de una
célula de Purkinje.

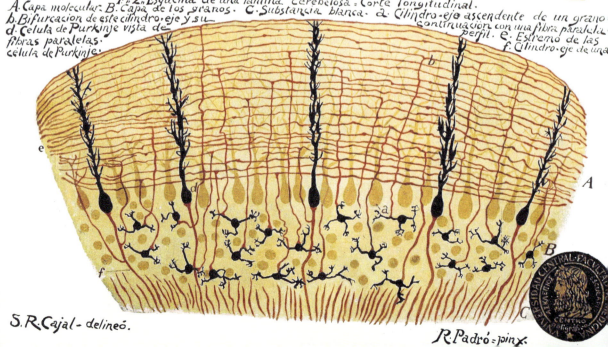

DIVIDED MIND

ZACHARY
DAVIS

I N 1840, WHEN HE WAS THIRTY years old, Louis Victor Leborgne suddenly lost the ability to speak. He was able to understand spoken language and could communicate somewhat through basic hand gestures, but his own verbal expression became limited to a single syllable: *tan*. His family admitted Leborgne to the psychiatric division of Bicêtre Hospital outside Paris in search of treatment, but the cause of his condition remained a mystery. Eventually his health declined, and he was seen by Pierre Paul Broca, a physician who had recently become interested in new hypotheses about the brain.

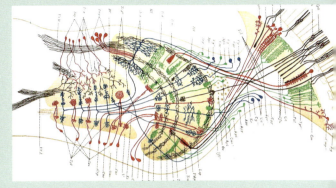

Santiago Ramón y Cajal

At the time, scientists were debating whether different areas of the brain performed separate functions or whether the brain, like the liver, was an undifferentiated lump that did one task. Broca was fascinated by this question and believed Leborgne's mysterious condition might hold the key. On April 17, 1861, just six days after first being examined by Dr. Broca, Leborgne died. Broca performed an autopsy and discovered a lesion in the left frontal lobe of Leborgne's brain. This finding was groundbreaking; it provided physical evidence for the localization of brain function, linking a specific region of the brain to specific speech disorders. Broca went on to examine more patients with similar speech loss and found consistent damage in the same location, which would later be known as Broca's area.

Broca's research was the first to suggest that different functions are localized in either the left or right hemisphere of the brain, a concept known as cerebral lateralization. But the leap from these early observations to a more nuanced understanding of how the two hemispheres work wouldn't come for another hundred years. In the 1940s, doctors discovered that for people suffering from severe epilepsy, one of the only effective treatments was a radical surgical procedure that severed the band of neural fibers (the corpus callosum) that connected the brain's two hemispheres. In the 1960s, CalTech neuropsychologist Robert

Sperry began conducting studies on patients who had undergone this procedure, intrigued by the prospect of testing the cognitive capabilities of each hemisphere independently. Sperry and his colleagues pioneered this "split-brain" research using ingenious experiments to discover that the left hemisphere was predominantly involved in linguistic, analytical, and logical tasks, while the right hemisphere excelled in spatial, intuitive, and holistic processing.

Along with helping Sperry win the Nobel Prize in 1981, this split-brain research also helped birth the popular notion that people can be categorized as either left-brained (logical and analytical) or right-brained (intuitive and creative). But the truth of how the brain works is more subtle and complex than an online self-help test tends to be. Rather than representing a simple dichotomy, the two hemispheres work together as a dynamic, flexible, and interconnected system. And the degree to which one hemisphere is engaged over the other can depend on the task at hand. For example, while language is generally a left-hemisphere function, the right hemisphere may be more engaged in understanding metaphors or emotional tones.

Nevertheless, the psychiatrist and philosopher Iain McGilchrist argues that hemispheric differences (or at least the values that they represent) are real and significant and are even in constant competition, vying for dominance in how we interpret and experience the world. In his 2009 book *The Master and His Emissary*, McGilchrist claims that we tend to view the right hemisphere as our fun, slightly unserious artsy friend who wears outrageously colorful outfits, and the left hemisphere as our three-piece-suit-wearing boss who does the important stuff like logic and problem-solving. But this gets the proper hierarchy all wrong. For McGilchrist, in an optimally functioning mind, the right hemisphere should be the master, holistically, intuitively, and imaginatively perceiving the world in a relational, interconnected manner. It can see the whole. By contrast, the left hemisphere has a more narrow perspective, good at analyzing parts, examining details, and completing specific tasks, but blind to the full picture. It should be the emissary, the servant.

But McGilchrist believes that in modern society, the emissary has usurped the master's role. In a process that began with the Enlightenment's passionate pursuit of instrumental reason and presentist preference for knowledge over wisdom, our culture has become imbalanced in favor of left-hemispheric ways of thinking: analytical, abstract, and focused on decontextualized parts rather than wholes. As a result, our perspective has become fragmented, and the values of efficiency, utility, and technical control have triumphed over the pursuit of meaning, connection, beauty, and holiness.

Much of the psychic and spiritual pain we feel is because we know in our hearts we have created an inhospitable home, a culture that doesn't support our deepest longings. As McGilchrist writes, "we should be appropriately skeptical of the left hemisphere's vision of a mechanistic world, an atomistic society, a world in which competition is more important than collaboration; a world in which nature is a heap of resource there for our exploitation, in which only humans count, and yet humans are only machines—not even very good ones, at that."[1] The truth, as the physicist David Böhm observed, is that the universe is not a collection of objects, but rather a web of relationships.

The consequences of being blind to the relational nature of reality can perhaps most clearly be seen by comparing industrial and traditional farming. Industrial farming approaches land as a resource to be used for maximum short-term profit and is usually marked by monoculture, heavy use of synthetic fertilizers and pesticides, and the pursuit of ever larger scale. Such practices often result in soil degradation, water pollution, reduced biodiversity, and impoverished rural communities.

In contrast, in traditional farming, the farm is cared for as a whole, with each component—water, soil, plants, animals, humans—considered a vital part and deserving of nurture and attention. Under this kind of holistic care, farms can provide perpetual abundance. As the farmer and writer Wendell Berry has written, "the farmer has put plants and animals into a relationship of mutual dependence, and must perforce be concerned for balance or symmetry . . . [for] the whole complex of problems whose proper solutions add up to health: the *health* of the soil, of plants and animals, of farm and farmer, of farm family and farm community, all involved in the same internested, interlocking pattern."[2]

Discerning the interlocking pattern that Berry describes is to see with a more expansive perspective. It is to begin to see as God does, with love and concern for the whole of creation, for each sparrow, for each soul. We have been called to bring forth Zion, to become "of one heart and one mind."[3] I don't believe that means that we think or feel in exactly the same way, but rather we live the truth that the flourishing of one requires the flourishing of all, that we are each beloved members of God's family, and that we are each wrapped up in the great shared story of Christ's redemption. It is our prayer that the writing and art in this issue offer glimpses of that broader vision and that together we join hands to build a new City of Holiness. In the process, we hope to find our "hearts knit together in unity and in love one towards another."[4] ✳

1. Iain McGilchrist, *The Master and His Emissary: The Divided Brain and the Making of the Western World* (New Haven: Yale University Press, 2009), xxvi.

2. Wendell Berry, "Solving for Pattern," in *The Gift of Good Land: Further Essays Cultural and Agricultural* (San Francisco: North Point Press, 1981), 137.

3. Moses 7:18.

4. Mosiah 18:21.

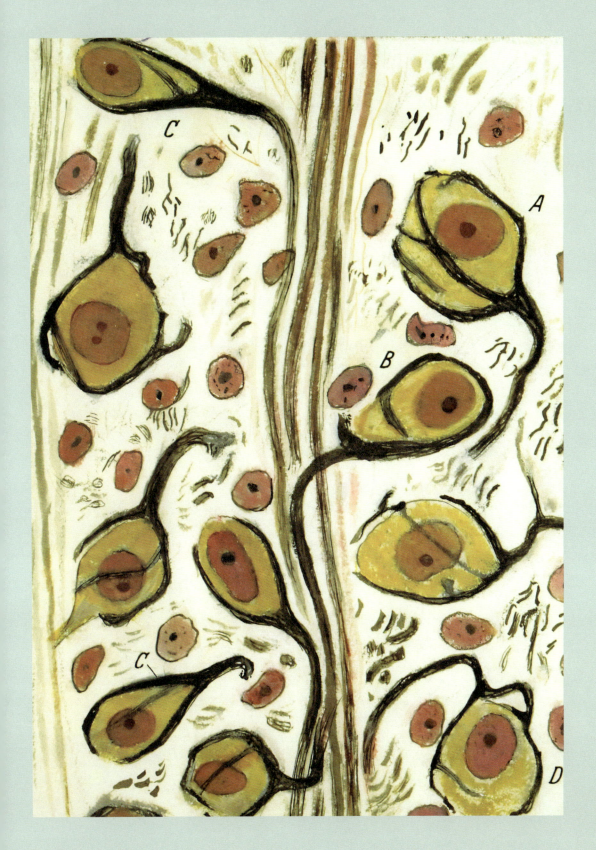

SPIRITUAL CARTOGRAPHY

Idolatry & Restoration

MATTHEW BOWMAN

A FEW MONTHS AGO, MY SISTER asked me to talk to a friend who had just learned that Joseph Smith's practice of polygamy left in its wake broken hearts, painful feelings, and for many a sense of betrayal. Over and over, she asked questions like: "Why have I never heard this at church? Is there any path for me to be a Mormon knowing what I know now? How can you, somebody who knows so much about the history of the Church, still go to church?"

I have talked with people who have come to doubt the reality of Noah's flood, people who are distressed by the Church's firm adherence to mid-twentieth-century gender norms, people troubled by Joseph Smith's marriages and use of a seer stone. Some have learned facts about early Church history that are disturbing. Others are bothered by the Church's positions on current social issues. Perhaps, most of all, these people feel lied to or deceived. They have learned things about the Church's past and present that don't jibe with what they believed it was, or even what members and leaders of the Church taught them.

Often, these people say that reconciliation is impossible, and that their questions must simply be lived with as a thorn in the side ("put on the shelf," as some say), or that the Church must be abandoned entirely. And sometimes, trying to solve these questions can only make the problem worse. For instance, if somebody comes to me with worries about Joseph Smith's plural marriage, providing the facts I've learned can be useful, but attempting to extrapolate from those facts how this person should feel may not.

There are many particular issues like these that trouble people about the Church. I've thought and read and written about many of them. But it's fruitless to play whack-a-mole like this endlessly. There is much pain in the Church's past, and of course there is, because there is pain and mistakes in anything humans do. There is a great deal of uncertainty embedded in being a religious person, and of course there is, because there is a great deal of uncertainty in being alive. The basic problem confronting many members of the Church is, I think, not that these things exist, but that many of us have convinced each other that mistakes and problems and uncertainty are dangerous to religion rather than inevitable.

Another way of putting this idea is that behind many of the particular problems that trouble Church members is a single major problem. It's an old problem, as old as the Bible itself. If the Israelites were God's chosen people, why would

> **Either way, the theory seems to be that mistakes and pain are a deviation from what the Church should be. The problem is that none of this is accurate.**

the Babylonians be allowed to destroy Jerusalem? If Joseph Smith were a prophet, why would he institute polygamy in a way that seemed guaranteed to inflict great emotional pain on his wife Emma? If Brigham Young (or Joseph Fielding Smith or any number of other leaders of the Church) were a prophet, why would he repeat common racist clichés to justify denying Black people full participation in the gospel, clichés that the Church today rejects?

One way of answering these problems is simply to say that God allows people to make mistakes, which is manifestly true. But that answer can seem unsatisfying. What's the point of a prophet if that person makes mistakes with the magnitude of Brigham Young's racism? How do we know when a prophet is or is not making a mistake?

Another way of answering the problems is to scramble to deny them, to defend the reputation of the Church and its leaders by shifting blame, downplaying error, insisting that when the Church's history is correctly understood, then pain and mistakes, when not minimized entirely, can be rationalized as necessary, part of God's plan.

Either way, the theory seems to be that mistakes and pain are a deviation from what the Church should be. The problem is that none of this is accurate. But the fact that it is not is, I think, its own sort of redemption.

MORONI'S PROMISE

Here's what I mean. When I entered graduate school, I had been inactive in the Church for nearly ten years. There were a lot of reasons for this, but most orbited around the fact that I didn't have the spiritual experiences I was told I should have. A devoted seminary teacher promised me

and the rest of my class that if we prayed about the Book of Mormon, God would grant us a burning in the bosom, which would be the Holy Spirit confirming to us the book was true.

I was an earnest and serious and anxious kid. I went home and read the Book of Mormon in a week. Then, with a distinct sense of nervousness and excitement, I knelt by my bed and prayed. And I stayed there on my knees for at least half an hour, hoping and waiting, and nothing happened, and nothing happened. And I was confused and a bit bereft. After a day or two I concluded that I must have done something wrong, so I decided to read the book again. I did, and I prayed about it again, and again nothing happened.

So I went to the seminary teacher, and he kindly asked me exactly the wrong question. Was I praying with a pure heart and real intent? I—a fairly naïve and earnest kid—was baffled. Six months or so later, I told my parents I didn't want to go to church anymore.

My confusion progressed to frustration and then to anger at that seminary teacher in particular and then at the Church in general. I was a particularly annoying sort of atheist for a while. (I think there's real pain in a lot of ex-religious people, and I despair seeing that pain curdle into the sort of snarky, tired zingers about God that I embraced.) And of course, that teacher could have been more sensitive.

But it's a mistake, I think, to see him as personally at fault. He was simply enacting broader patterns he was taught. He was struggling to reconcile the effortless and simple universe he had been taught to believe in with the grimy and limping reality we actually live in.

It's those patterns, more so than the particular issues that they generate, that I want to examine. These are patterns of certainty, of overconfidence, patterns that envision the religious life as a great mechanism that works like an assembly line, piecing together a predictable series of parts—good actions here, right belief there—to produce expected results.

Or to take another metaphor, that seminary teacher had been taught that religion is a map to salvation. God has given us a set of instructions on how to get there and has designated certain people or texts to pass them on. Set aside precisely what those instructions might be—accepting Jesus, obeying his commandments, achieving karmic balance, participating in sacraments and ordinances like baptism—for our purposes this matters less than the fact that there are instructions. There is a map. Under this definition, religion is the word we use to name the process of following the map God gives you.

That is what that seminary teacher was trying to accomplish. Learn about the map, follow the map. If the road he pointed me down led to a dead end, the problem was with the one who followed the map, not the map itself. He and I had both forgotten that the map is not the territory.

MAPS

The scholar of religion Jonathan Z. Smith popularized the phrase "map is not territory" to warn us about confusing our descriptions of a thing for the thing itself. Believing that the map is the territory can fool us into mistaking that we know the land far better than we do. We might confuse the clear, straight lines and dots on the paper for what the land before us actually is: roads, cities, hills, trees, rivers, valleys.

That is what I had done. I had studied the map we had been given, a map produced by a late twentieth-century curriculum committee directed and inspired by late twentieth-century general authorities, and concluded that it contained the entirety of what my religion could be. In the particular approach that particular seminary teacher offered me, the entire thing was useless.

Now, of course I did this. I was a teenager.

I used to teach a course called "Introduction to the Study of Religion." It was not a World Religions course—a march through Judaism and Islam and Buddhism and so on. Instead, we asked what made some things religion and other things not. When I asked my students what religion was, they tended to generalize from Christianity. Religions believe in God, are about going to heaven, have moral codes, and so on. But then I would bring up Zen Buddhism and ask them if

Emilia Wing

Emilia Wing

As for that seminary teacher—I broke his map. He didn't know what to do, so he struggled to locate me on the map, rather than considering that the territory underneath the map, where I was wandering, might be something different than he imagined it to be. His map of Mormonism was a version where the part of the Book of Mormon the Church's missionary program started calling "Moroni's promise" in the twentieth century would always work the same way.

But, as Jonathan Z. Smith or any other historian of religion might point out, the Church has not always used that passage in that way, and it may stop doing so in the future. Or, to extrapolate even more, the Church has embraced dozens of ways throughout its history to talk about how somebody might have a spiritual experience, and it has inevitably discarded some and will inevitably embrace many more. That that particular map did not work for me did not mean that there are not other maps available.

The point here is not that maps are bad and we should pay attention to the territory instead. Nor is the point that each individual has their own map and we shouldn't try to impose them on each other. Neither of those things are true.

The point is this: maps are inevitable. We need them. We borrow them from those we trust, either consciously or implicitly—teachers, leaders, friends, our social media feed—and cobble them together from Sunday School lessons and what our parents teach us. Your map shares a lot with those of your friends and family. You share maps on social media and over the kitchen table and start to build them together, naming the various landmarks so you can all recognize them: "feeling the Spirit," "shelf breaking." The landmarks point you to various endpoints, of having a testimony or building a relationship with God. The map helps you make sense of what your life looks like.

But even though maps are inevitable, we have to adopt them with awareness that they are not territory, which is another way of saying that in another time, or another place, that teacher and I might have thought somewhat differently about what feeling the Spirit is. Our maps are born of a collision between absolute eternity and our

it was a religion. Because they'd heard it called a religion, they usually said yes, whereupon I'd point out that Zen Buddhism does not have a deity and does not describe a heaven. This tended to confuse everybody.

They did the same thing I had. For them, "religion" could be measured by the Protestant Christianity most of them were raised with.

Jonathan Z. Smith used the comparison of the map and the territory to illustrate the problem of defining "religion." He argued that humans tend to overgeneralize about religion, to try to reduce what religion is to something familiar that matches our expectations. But always, as we study the past or the present of human religious experience, we'll find something that scrambles our definitions.

Maps are our definitions of religion. They're always marked by the culture that we live in. The territory is that vast swath of country that overflows any given moment. The territory of Christianity includes both Russell M. Nelson and St. Peter, both Joan of Arc and Eliza R. Snow. What sort of sacrament meeting would satisfy all of them?

particular time and culture and place. And eventually we'll come to the edge of one map and need to find another to continue. That's normal.

This is to say that it's common and easy to assume that the way of understanding what it means to be religious that we were raised with is the only way, and that if that way doesn't work, we have to give it up. Or it's easy to assume that this way is a map and that giving it up is abandoning all maps for the territory itself. But that's not true. It's maps, in a sense, all the way down.

That the Church has changed its maps in the past and will change in the future does not actually mean that it is not "true"—instead, it means that it is what the Doctrine and Covenants calls "true and living." The problem is not that the Church changes its maps, because the Church has a lot of maps. The problem is when we freeze a single map and pretend that it is the same map that Moses, Peter, and Joseph Smith used. Or the problem is believing that we can somehow get away from maps entirely. We can't. When we do that, we're committing idolatry.

IDOLATRY

What's idolatry? Simply put, idolatry is worshiping things that aren't God, like the idols—golden calves and statues of Zeus and so on—that people in the Bible are always going on about.

But idolatry is more than that. Martin Luther said that "whatever your heart clings to and relies upon, that is your God."[1] Idolatry tempts you to invest a fallible and limited human idea or institution or practice with absolute faith and confidence. Idolatry is the child of certainty. It leads you to reject the possibility that you might be wrong. It happens whenever you come to believe so fully in your convictions that you come to assume, even unconsciously, that your beliefs are immune to the flaws and limitations that history and culture places upon all of us. It's believing your map has no edges.

Everything in this world will at some point break under the pressure of your faith and trust. Everything—every ideology, every institution, every person—will reach questions it cannot answer and problems it cannot solve. For some

people a political party becomes an idol; for other people a particular writer; for others, it's being cool or Bernie Sanders or Taylor Swift or the Constitution. All of these have their own cliff's edge.

Because we worry about our own flaws, we invest power in things that we hope will protect us from failure. We project confidence, we feign certainty, we embrace righteous anger. We believe in simple answers. And then we grow vehement about defending the things we have invested in, since deep down the anxiety remains, because money or ideology or doing this thing or that won't help you fix all the ways this world is broken. It can't.

Idolatry destroys because it is a product of anxiety that only feeds that anxiety in turn. Idolatry is like scratching a mosquito bite; it is satisfying in the moment, but in the long run the underlying problem only grows more inflamed.

Idolatry is refusing to admit the possibility that your map is not the territory.

I think our religious lives are a contest between restoration and idolatry; between pretending that our maps are the territory and coming to understand that religion is actually the process of swapping out, redrawing, adding detail to—restoring, in a word—the maps we have had in the past.

Doing these things is not an embarrassing error or an inevitable mistake. Rather, the beating heart of the religious life is the consciousness that all maps are finite. They resonate with the reality of territory, but full perception of that place lies inevitably, as we live, beyond us. The purpose of religion is to help us understand that we will travel from map to map throughout our lives, with our eye upon a perfect territory we may never fully inhabit in this life, but nonetheless can imagine and aspire to.

The answer to idolatry, then, is not cynicism or doubt. It's charity. Charity is the willingness to place your faith in things even with the knowledge that they'll at some point fail. We can develop the capacity to forgive and help to mend what will eventually break, because these things contain goodness and truth, and your expectations were not unrealistic in the first place.

The light of human history shows us that religion changes over time. Recognizing that the map is not the territory brings the wisdom to see that change is what religion is for. Religion is less about belief than it is about action. It is about abandoning the false certainty of idolatry for the act of restoration.

RESTORATION

One way of imagining restoration is to think of it like a light switch. It is on or it is off. When it is on, the Church exists in essentially the same way, whether it be AD 38 or AD 2023. When it is off, history happens. Roman Catholicism and Protestantism and Eastern Orthodoxy—all of these religions run by human beings—are the products of historical development and change over time, human beings making decisions in the context of their culture. But all of those things are suspended at the moment of restoration. The Church does not exist in history; the Church exists only in truth.

But I think this is a bad way to imagine what restoration is. Instead of an accomplishment, I think that restoration is an effort. It is a way of acting, not something that happens to you.

The central idea of Christianity and of our Restoration is this: Jesus comes to us in history. Jesus left eternity to join a particular moment in a particular place. He told parables based upon the lives of rural Mediterranean peasants that would be meaningful to those who heard

Emilia Wing

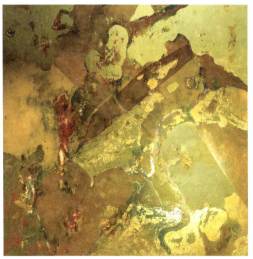

them—and many of them, quite frankly, mean far less to us than they did to those people who eventually wrote them down, just as the parable of the bicycle means a great deal to modern Americans but would mean little to them. Jesus had no dental care. He wore the clothes and ate the food that those around him did. He died in a bloody and authoritarian punishment. His life was unimaginable to virtually any member of the Church living in the United States today.

But then, we believe, he came here too. He spoke to a common farm boy. He told that boy to make Jesus comprehensible to people in that time and that place. Restoration, like Jesus himself, is incarnation. It is a translation of the absolute and the divine into the particulars of a specific time and place and people. And in so doing, the divine casts what seems normal to us in a new light, forcing us to reconsider our beliefs and assumptions.

Jesus comes to us as much as we go to him. And that means that seeking restoration does not mean simply endlessly replicating a particular sort of Christianity because we imagine it is the one correct way to be a Christian.

But this gestures to a paradox. If religion is always changing, is there in fact something called "religion" in the first place? What does "restoration" mean if it looks different in any time and situation? There are a number of ways to answer this, but for our purposes we will go with one.

The theologian Paul Tillich said that religion might be best defined as the human attempt to venerate and gesture to things of "ultimate concern."[2] Religion derives from our belief in, sense of, and hunger for the certainty and perfection that doesn't exist in our lives, but which we can imagine and which we hope for. Tillich says that this perfection is what God is. And we can sense and imagine perfection, Tillich teaches, because of the spark of divinity in us.

That spark helps us to imagine what the world and ourselves might be like. What we would be like having fully overcome the "natural man"—our seemingly inborn instincts toward selfishness and self-preservation and anger and revenge. It can also help us imagine what the world that Jesus calls us to live in might be like:

> **Religion derives from our belief in, sense of, and hunger for the certainty and perfection that doesn't exist in our lives, but which we can imagine and which we hope for.**

a world of charity and justice, a place where God wipes away all tears.

And yet, because our lives are constantly incomplete, our attempts to touch that perfection are always incomplete. Being religious means trying to touch it again and again, in different times, places, and situations. And that means we have to do it in different ways. We have to dig into the resources that we have and try to define anew what we want to be in every generation.

This idea, of course, poses a danger. As the epistle to the Ephesians puts it, we may risk being blown about by every wind of doctrine, adapting religion to the culture around it and stripping it of its capacity to imagine different worlds. Nobody ever thinks they're being blown about by a wind of doctrine. Instead, we take things for granted. We assume that the world our friends or parents or the people we follow on social media show us is true.

That is what the idea of restoration should help us avoid. Just as, on the one hand, we should see in Jesus how religion's vitality, energy, and capacity to change human lives comes from its adaptability, we can also see in Jesus its persistence.

The most vital religious traditions in human history are those that give expression and meaning to the reality of change, defying idolatry. But at the same time, they need to be deeply connected to the accumulated lessons of a tradition.

They bind change to their identity. They accord respect to their past and that identity.

Roman Catholics call this process "ressourcement," a French word meaning, literally, a "return to the sources." What Catholics mean by that is that as the world develops and human cultures change, their faith constantly returns to itself, explores its own resources, and finds in them new answers for problems that earlier Catholics had not considered because those problems did not yet exist.

In so doing, they avoid idolatry and embrace restoration.

THE CHURCH AND HISTORY

The certainty that idolatry offers is tempting. It's often reproduced in the teaching institutions of the Church, as it builds the maps its members seek. Certainty fosters commitment. It makes them strong, but it also leaves them brittle. When people who have been raised on certainty experience their first dose of uncertainty, it can leave them dazed and wobbling. This is the set of experiences we have come to call the "faith crisis."

And all too often, people struggling with the fragility of certainty simply reproduce the absolutist logic of idolatry. It is perfect and good or it is wrong and bad. Each proposition implies the truth of the next. If your seminary teacher failed you, the Church is corrupt. If you think the Book of Mormon has truth in it, you must accept that conference talks are revelation. And so on.

This is fundamentalism. It's important to define the word. "Fundamentalism" is often used today to mean virtually any religious belief or activity that seems extreme to the person who uses the word. But we should not use the term as a slur. Instead it's worth examining precisely what those people who proudly embraced the term meant by it. The word was coined by Protestants who explicitly opposed the idea that religion might change over time.

Threatened by modernity, they produced a modernity of their own: their belief system, fundamentalism, attempted to reduce religion to a science. Water freezes at 32 degrees Fahrenheit, and always has. Similarly, fundamentalists argued that their interpretations of scripture were clear and verifiable. They denied that religion is affected by history. Fundamentalism is the opposite of restoration.

Latter-day Saints were influenced by fundamentalist thought in the mid-twentieth century. And many still feel its touch. These are those

Church members who fear that if, for instance, Joseph Smith believed something because he was influenced by his time and culture rather than because he knew it via revelation, his status as a prophet will be called into question. Or they assume that, for instance, because Nephi in the Book of Mormon refers to the "books of Moses," a common ancient term for the first five books of the Hebrew Bible, those books must indeed be written by Moses. The idea that Nephi might simply be incorrect seems dangerous.

Fear is the right word. Fundamentalism promotes fear. Its ideas sow worry that God needs defense, and that leads to hyperbole. Fundamentalism turns religion into an idol, a plaster statue, a God who is terribly fragile, easily broken if knocked off of the shelf.

Fundamentalism sacrifices what can be most useful and powerful about religion: its capacity to challenge every assumption and gesture constantly toward further possibility of change, rebirth, and renewal.

One primary fundamentalist strategy is to claim that only fundamentalism is "real" religion; that nonfundamentalist versions of faith are corrupt or worldly. And oddly enough, many who reject fundamentalist religion still assent to the premise of that dichotomy. They feel burned by fundamentalism but argue that nonfundamentalist religion is all compromise and "mental gymnastics"—that fundamentalism is genuine religion, and therefore religion in total is stultifying. That argument can feel compelling because some people who abandon faith retain fundamentalist ways of thinking about religion, even if they have abandoned particular fundamentalist beliefs. They continue to subscribe to the idol of fundamentalist religion even as they claim to reject it.

Restoration, on the other hand, can crack the window and let light in. There are resources in the Church's history and theology, in its practice of restoration, that allow for our own ressourcement that can render our religion more meaningful and powerful.

Fundamentalism describes faith as knowledge. It pressures us to say that we "know" things are true and stakes a great deal on whether or not they are verifiably accurate. It creates binaries—but binaries do not reflect the reality of lived religion. A comprehensive and specific map can seem certain, but it remains simply a map. Our constant groping for a map that better fits our sense of the territorym, our constant sense that we must progress and develop and adapt the restoration—that is what gives faith meaning and value. A binary cannot sustain that reality.

In the logic of restoration, though, cognitive knowledge, or the things we know by thinking, is subordinate to the knowledge we gain through relationships. Richard Bushman has written that Joseph Smith hungered for family.[3] The trauma he endured as son of parents downwardly mobile, whose economic catastrophes moved the family restlessly across early America, who lost young siblings to disease—all of this drove him to consider religion less as a source of cognitive knowledge than of experiential knowledge.

Joseph Smith was less concerned to know his lost brother was waiting in heaven than, simply, to know his lost brother again. And thus, the religious world he imagined was one in which the centrifugal economic and social forces tearing his family apart were stilled, and human beings were knit together again. His religion was a way of describing a deep truth about human nature: that we are not, fundamentally, individuals tasked with self-creation, but that we are social beings, shaped by those around us more than by ourselves.

In his lifetime he expressed this impulse through polygamy, the gathering of the Church, and sealing. In our lifetimes the Church expresses this impulse through celebration of the Western nuclear family. And understanding that religion is something deeply marked by history and culture allows us to see the fundamental hunger lying behind both of these expressions—to perceive them as different, but of a kind. Liberation, authenticity, finding who we are is not a project of disassociation and separation. Rather, liberation is recognizing our belonging—that we are shaped by others, by our communities, and by our families—and in that recognition finding reconciliation with ourselves and with others.

We, each of us, from Joseph Smith to Russell Nelson to my bishop to myself, are marked by our culture as much as the Church itself is. So is

Emilia Wing

the cast that our families might take and how we interpret what they are. These are maps.

Of course, this is not the single right way to interpret the Church and its history. The point is that there is no single right way. The history of Mormonism gives us a vast set of ideas and inheritances, traditions and revelations for encountering God. Some may work best in some times and places; others will work best in others.

The point is this: God is not a concept, an idea, something frozen in time. God is a person, and thus encountering God is not about mastering a rigorous set of doctrines, but understanding and trusting in the bonds of a relationship that will inevitably change over time, just as your relationship with those you trust most will change over time.

The heartbeat of that relationship is what religion is: something living, something that grows and evolves, something that flourishes in different ways in different times and places.

The fact that religion is living can give hope. Jesus is calling in every language, in every time. Having faith is having the hope to live in the world that being religious promises is possible, and acting on that hope—to be willing to turn your back on the temptation of sterile idolatry and to plunge into the possibility and blessed reality of change. ✵

1. Martin Luther, "Large Catechism," in *The Book of Concord: The Confessions of the Evangelical Lutheran Church*, ed. Robert Kolb and Timothy J. Wengert, trans. Charles Arand et al. (Minneapolis: Fortress, 2000), 386.

2. Paul Tillich, *Theology of Culture* (London: Oxford University Press). 6-7.

3. Richard Bushman, "The Inner Joseph Smith," *Journal of Mormon History*, vol. 32, no. 1 (Spring 2006), 65–81.

THROUGH THE WARDROBE

Inhabiting the Divine Story

LIZ BUSBY

I HAVE BEEN A STUDENT OF C. S. Lewis for as long as I have been a reader. His Chronicles of Narnia were some of the first books I stumbled haltingly through when I first transitioned from reading phonetically to reading for pleasure. As I hid in closets and behind couches reading my mother's 1970s editions, I longed to go to Narnia, this land where children became heroes by showing virtue and courage. There was just something about being in Narnia that felt immediately right to my soul. I completely failed to notice any of the Christian symbolism of the books. When it was pointed out to me while I was still quite young, I felt as if I had been tricked, that the adventures I had enjoyed were somehow cheapened because they were "really" about something else.

My thoughts about symbolism have changed somewhat over the years. While studying literature as an undergraduate, I realized that only the poorest symbols were merely one thing standing in for another. The symbols crafted by the greatest writers stood for entire stories and went on to become used in other texts as shorthand for a larger experience: Oedipus Rex, Hamlet, and Atticus Finch, for example. In this way, fiction often captures truths greater than the factual realities of nonfiction.

However, my mind was still tainted with the idea that the Narnian Chronicles were the other sort of fiction, a transparent allegory with poor and incoherent worldbuilding meant for children who didn't know to expect better. Perhaps some of this thinking was borrowed from Philip Pullman, author of the rival children's series *His Dark Materials* who famously dismissed Narnia as "propaganda."[1] But whatever way it happened, I came to believe that though Lewis was a first-rate apologist and critic, he was a poor fiction writer. Oh, certainly, *The Screwtape Letters* and *The Great Divorce* were excellent in their own way, but they merely proved the point that Lewis was much better at allegory than he was at genuine fiction writing. Of course, I avoided actually rereading the Chronicles of Narnia to find out if this hypothesis was true. I didn't want to trample on what remained of the magic I had felt as a child.

When a recent perusal of an audiobook sale turned up Michael Ward's *Planet Narnia: The Seven Heavens in the Imagination of C. S. Lewis*, I was intrigued enough to add it to my library. A revolutionary book in Lewis studies published in

Jessica Sarah Beach

2007, *Planet Narnia* held out for me the hope of an innovative interpretation of the novels, one that might restore my childhood experience. Yet I dithered and delayed. I was afraid that the argument wouldn't hold together, that I would once again be let down.

The moment for reading finally came when our family was on a Church history road trip, driving from Utah to New York and back again. In the middle of the Great Plains on a Latter-day pilgrimage to the Kirtland Temple, I found myself driving without anything to listen to. My kids were all busy with video games, and my husband was reading on his Kindle. I flipped through a few podcasts, tried to pick up the work of classic literature that I'd been slogging through for months, then put on the speculative fiction novel I had recently started, but nothing seemed satisfying. As I furtively scrolled through my audiobook catalog while keeping one eye on the unchanging highway surrounded by corn fields, I decided to give *Planet Narnia* a shot. It seemed a strange choice even to me—who listens to literary criticism to stay awake?—but I was desperate for something, so I pushed play.

The Kirtland Temple, the first of the Restoration, can seem alien to even the most experienced temple attender, as different from our typical temple experience as other temples are from our Sunday worship. This temple has no creation room, no celestial room; it feels more like a church than a temple. I wonder if the early Saints were confused about why they were commanded to build it. They came from a culture that assumed the need for a temple had ended with Christ's resurrection. Were they as baffled by this first temple as many Latter-day Saints are by their first temple experience?

Attending the temple for the first time is a threshold moment in the life of a Latter-day Saint. When I was preparing for my endowment, people around me began sharing stories of how different the temple would be. A sister in my parents' ward had come out of her endowment feeling so bewildered that she immediately went back in for a second session, determined to show the devil that he couldn't make her doubt. My future father-in-law warned me that many people felt strange about how different it was from our typical worship services and that I should go into it without preconceptions.

I was surprised to find that my experience was completely different from anything I'd been led to expect. In the temple, I felt at home.

In sacrament meetings, talks seemed to endlessly repeat basic principles, adding little to a generic outline of the gospel. In Sunday School classes, people simplified the scriptures until they were mere outlines pointing to a moral lesson. But the endowment skipped this sort of direct teaching. It focused instead on an experience, a story with symbols. Just as when reading a novel, in the endowment, we are asked to ally ourselves with the protagonists of a story—the story of humanity—and accept their experience as our own. As Adam and Eve experience the creation and the paradise of Eden, their fall and their redemption, we experience it along with them. The temple let me sit in that story without feeling a need to explain anything. Indeed, I became a part of it.

For similar reasons, I always loved the war chapters of the Book of Mormon because they let me sit with the characters and their motivations. I was baffled when others complained that there was so little of value that they had to slog through the second half of Alma and all of Helaman to reach 3 Nephi on the other side. For me, those chapters were the most narrative—and therefore the best—chapters in scripture. Sure, I couldn't practically apply Nephite war strategy in my life in any but the most metaphorical ways. But I could glimpse the twisted logic of self-justification through Zerahemnah's speech and feel through Moroni the power of righteous anger and the abashedness of finding it misplaced. Those chapters were aflame with an atmosphere of utterly crucial moral choices. I learned more about living a moral life by breathing their air than by any sermon contained in the book because I could learn, if not from my own experience, then at least from secondhand ones.

We're more likely to enjoy this kind of immersive story in a movie theater or the pages of a book than we are on our spiritual journey—perhaps because we're more likely to consume pop culture stories all at once, whereas our experiences of the sacred texts are meted out in weekly installments over the course of years. Few of us are binge-reading the scriptures, and even fewer of us are experiencing the scriptures as its intended genre of story or poem rather than a book of doctrine and wisdom. As C. S. Lewis put it in *An Experiment in Criticism*, his analysis

I was surprised to find that my experience was completely different from anything I'd been led to expect. In the temple, I felt at home.

of different ways of reading, we are more likely to "use" the scriptures to further our own thoughts than to "receive" them on their own terms. The opportunities to really surrender ourselves to the text, as Lewis says attentive readers must do, seem to be few and far between.

Was it always this way? No doubt there has always been proof-texting and inspirational reading, but the early Saints seemed to have understood the importance of inhabiting stories better than we do now. A year ago, when recent changes to the temple ceremony made me curious about past adjustments, I picked up Devery S. Anderson's *Development of LDS Temple Worship, 1846–2000: A Documentary History*. A compilation of diary entries, letters, First Presidency notes, and Church handbooks concerning the temple, the book shows the evolution of our understanding over time. One thread in particular I noticed was that it was not until recently that leaders began to comment on the difficulty of teaching young Church members to understand the temple.[2] Later, these concerns become a large part of the discourse, but in the early documents, Church leaders instead worry about keeping the Saints from joining other secret societies and prioritizing them over the temple. It seems to me that the prevalence of things like freemasonry in the American culture of the time gave the early Saints a framework for understanding the symbolic experience of the temple that we have no parallel for today.

Except when we talk about stories.

* *
*
* * *
* .

This is where Michael Ward's analysis of the Chronicles of Narnia comes back in. The type of fantasy fiction that C. S. Lewis and J. R. R. Tolkien wrote has come to be referred to as "mythopoeic fiction." In mythopoeic fiction, the author acts through narrative to create a new mythology, a new symbolism, which has spiritual significance both to the characters and to the readers of the story. This type of fiction is deeper than an allegory; each character doesn't just stand for some attribute, enacting a moralistic tale. When mythopoeic stories succeed, they are as resonant as those of authentic mythology.

As I drove my family down the highway towards the historic Kirtland Temple, Michael Ward's analysis opened to me his version of the mythopoeic meaning of Narnia. If this wasn't exactly the same wonder I had felt as a child, it was certainly like unto it. In *Planet Narnia*, Ward argues that the series was crafted to renew the medieval symbolism of the seven planets of the

> ## Perhaps the whole goal of the endowment is to experience the inherent quality of this mortal journey—to help us see, or more importantly feel, the bigger picture that God has for our lives.

medieval cosmos. This symbolic structure for the universe—which in turn was a repurposing of Greek and Roman mythology by medieval Christians—was being lost in modernity's more scientific ways of looking at the universe. Lewis felt our modern imaginations were poorer for the loss of these potent symbols, and so, Ward argues, he set about constructing a new version of these symbols for the modern imagination, reforging their meanings in the same way as they had been reframed by Christian scholars of old.

Rather than depicting the gods and the planets they symbolize directly, as Lewis did in his poem

"The Planets" and in his science fiction trilogy,[3] Ward argues that the Chronicles instead attempt to bathe the reader in the overall symbolic atmosphere of each of the planets. Lewis himself used various terms to capture this idea of a symbolic atmosphere in his own scholarship—"'a state or quality'; 'flavour or atmosphere'; 'smell or taste'; 'mood'; 'quiddity'"[4]—but Ward coins a new term for this writing technique as Lewis wields it. He calls it "donegality" after a quote from a letter Lewis wrote on the subject referencing a region in Ireland that Lewis loved:

> Lovers of romances go back and back to such stories in the same way we go "back to a fruit for its taste; to an air for . . . what? for *itself*; to a region for its whole atmosphere—to Donegal for its Donegality and London for its Londonness. It is notoriously difficult to put these tastes into words."[5]

In Ward's parlance, donegality means "a spirit that the author consciously sought to conjure, but which was designed to remain implicit in the matter of the text."[6]

In other words, each of the Narnia books explores the relationship between man and God through one of the medieval "seven heavens," all spiritually showing different sides of the divine nature, with an atmosphere that would evoke the same symbolism that medieval people felt at the mention of Mars or Saturn. The goal was not to teach about these symbols but to write a world and a story that would allow modern readers to experience and thus understand them.

For me, driving down that midwestern highway, Ward's explication of the spirit of the first Narnia book, *The Lion, the Witch, and the Wardrobe*, struck like a thunderbolt—aptly, since Ward's symbolic ruler of the novel is the spirit of Jupiter, otherwise known as Jove or Zeus. In medieval thought, he is the king of the gods; his spirit is one of benevolence and plenty, of joviality, the kingdom at peace and the banquet table prepared for his loyal followers. Ward was first tipped off to a possible connection by a line describing Jove in Lewis's poem "The Planets," which reads like a plot summary of the first Narnia book: "of wrath

Jessica Sarah Beach

ended / and woes mended, of winter passed / And guilt forgiven." Others have remarked that seeing the book through this lens makes sudden sense of one of Lewis's most cited egregious errors against believability: the presence of Father Christmas in a fantasy world of dryads and fauns. He is the ultimate modern embodiment of kingly celebration, of peace and plenty, the spirit of Jove, and so his place in the story makes sense symbolically, though Tolkien objected to his presence from a worldbuilding perspective.

But this was only a small piece of the understanding brought by seeing *The Lion, the Witch, and the Wardrobe* through the lens of Jupiter. As Michael Ward explained the various symbols of Jupiter present in the novel, I understood the story in a way I had never seen it before—or at least, in a way I hadn't seen since immersing myself in it as a first grader. Focusing on the kingly aspects of the plot suddenly reveals the journey of the four Pevensie children as one of divine ascent. Lucy and Edmund both fall into the land of Narnia by partaking of forbidden food (tea with the double-crossing faun Tumnus and the White Witch's Turkish delight), leading them into a confrontation with all that is wrong with this fallen world. From there, the children progress first by learning about Aslan, then by meeting him and committing to aid him in his recovery of Narnia. After they are redeemed from their fallen state by an atonement, they devote their very lives to the recovery of Narnia. In the end, through their faithfulness to Aslan, they are crowned kings and queens to rule under him in benevolence and peace.

I suddenly realized that the story described through the essence of Jove began to sound exactly like the stages of the endowment.

Was the reason I felt at home in the temple because of the stories I had read as a child? Narnia, among other heroic fantasy novels, taught me this pattern of ascent towards the divine, popularized by Joseph Campbell as the hero's journey. A person naturally started as an ignorant farm boy or girl, fell into a world of evil almost by accident, and gradually learned through experience and commitment to become the hero that the gods needed to fulfill their plans. Is it possible that so many are confused by the temple because we are so used to a religious environment that focuses on an analytic search for meaning rather than on the experience of divine growth? I began to see that the temple might not be about learning specific doctrines or specific knowledge, in spite of the tendency to focus on the sacred tokens and signs acquired there. Perhaps the whole goal of the endowment is to experience the inherent quality of this mortal journey—to help us see, or more importantly feel, the bigger picture that God has for our lives.

As my family pulled into Kirtland and onto the street where the temple sits, I was awed by the

Jessica Sarah Beach

humbleness of the building that represented the beginning of this experience for the Latter-day Saints. Though the Kirtland Temple never saw the administration of the modern endowment, it is where this holy atmosphere started. The sense of scale, captured by the endowment, was first present here, where a group of converts strove to accomplish in a small community that same feat which took medieval people centuries: the building of a sacred structure to give people the atmosphere of the divine.

In the end, it doesn't matter whether you buy that Lewis intentionally crafted the Narnia books with the seven heavens in mind or you think that

Ward has merely stumbled upon an interesting way to reread the series. The intentionality (or not) of the structure doesn't take away from the experience of the novels. After all, as a review of Ward's work noted, "children are not carried away by Lewis's plots, still less by his Christian allegories. What stays with them, rather, is the imagery: a faun carrying his umbrella through the snow, a lantern in the wilderness, a statue coming to life."[7] Similarly, perhaps we don't need to spend our time analyzing the endowment, trying to come to conclusions about what is symbolic and what those symbols mean. Perhaps the best way to understand the temple is

to simply exist within the experience, to consider ourselves as if we were Adam and Eve. Maybe, more than any direct doctrine or critical message, this is what the temple wants from us: a feeling, an atmosphere, a taste of our Heavenly Father's hopes for his children, an emanation from our heavenly home. ✳

1. Philip Pullman, "The Dark Side of Narnia," *Guardian*, October 1, 1998.

2. The first instance I found was from President N. Eldon Tanner, recorded in an entry in President David O. McKay's diary in 1966. This is based on a cursory reading, so I beg the readers' forgiveness if I have missed or mischaracterized the historical record. See Devery S. Anderson, ed., *The Development of LDS Temple Worship, 1846–2000: A Documentary History* (Salt Lake City: Signature Books, 2011), location 8269.

3. Though this series is without an official title, it is often referred to as the Space trilogy or the Ransom trilogy (after its main character). The second novel, *Perelandra*, is widely regarded as the best of the series and features a science fictional version of the Fall narrative that takes place on Venus.

4. Michael Ward, *Planet Narnia: The Seven Heavens in the Imagination of C. S. Lewis* (Oxford: Oxford University Press. 2008), 16.

5. Ward, *Planet Narnia*, 16.

6. Ward, *Planet Narnia*, 75.

7. Daniel Hannan, quoted in "Donegality," *New York Times*, September 24, 2010.

THE FULLNESS OF GOD

TERRYL GIVENS

ONE OF THE MOST BLOODSTAINED debates in Christian history was over the relationship of Jesus Christ to God the Father. Was he fully equal? Subordinate? Made by God or co-eternal with God? The Nicene creed (AD 325) declared the full equality, the "consubstantiality," of Father and Son—but the questions continued to be violently contested for many decades to come, especially in the Eastern empire. Much more was at stake in the debates than the abstract question of divine equality. Perhaps most critical for believers was (and is) the question, was the Incarnation of Jesus Christ—a being who suffered and wept, who both craved and knew love and friendship—a temporary setting aside of divinity, or the fullest possible revelation of that divinity? In historic Christianity, it is most often believed that "the king 'empties' himself, becoming a servant only for the duration of Jesus' brief ministry and the sacrifice of the cross, but his true being is as almighty king."[1] Others have seen the life and ministry of Jesus as an absolutely accurate reflection of the fullness of the Father. No question has greater impact on how we understand the nature of God. And Christian history reveals no consensus on the answer to that question.

Early Christians, almost without exception, saw Jesus as subordinate to the Father.[2] They also proclaimed that Jesus brought an astonishing new understanding of God. Before the love that was made concrete and effable in Jesus, mused a first-century convert, "what men had any inkling of who God is?"[3] Ignatius and Irenaeus made similar declarations. Maximus the Confessor agreed some centuries later: "through his flesh he made manifest to men *the Father whom they did not know.*"[4] Jesus's life of compassion, nonviolence, forgiveness, and selfless sacrifice created radically new ways of thinking about God's power and dominion. For early Saints, forgiveness, mercy, selflessness, humility—these were not temporary expedients for surviving in a hostile Roman empire; they were the authentic way of emulating

and acquiring "the divine nature." Jesus was not just showing the way; he *was* the way.

But human constructions of power and justice and authority and kingship have persistently pushed against Jesus's revolutionary gospel. Human passion for fairness and retribution, for validation and vindication, have often led Christians to see Jesus's repudiation of the crown in favor of the manger, his refusal of sovereignty in favor of loving service, as a mere ploy, a role he temporarily assumed (this has become the doctrine of *kenosis*).[5] Even devout Christians can sing hymns that anticipate with sacred schadenfreude a return in triumph of him who first came in humility, perhaps forgetting that his conquest of death and sin through love was his triumph.

A church in Ravenna marvelously but tragically bears witness to the church's insistence that God embodies all those trappings of power and prestige from which Jesus tried to wean us. In the early sixth century, Arian Christians in Sant'Apollinare Nuovo created some of the most stunning mosaics to survive in the modern world. Jesus is depicted through the various stages of his life: as a beardless youth healing the sick and raising Lazarus; a more mature Jesus sups with his disciples and is betrayed by Judas.

A few decades later, conquering Nicaean Christians removed some mosaics and added their own: an enthroned Christ in majesty. Elsewhere in Ravenna, images of Christ in a soldier's garb appear. The figure of Christ Pantocrator—Christ the All-Powerful—becomes pervasive in church art. Gradually, systematically, increasingly, Jesus has been reinscribed in all those forms of power and status that his life bore witness against. A Jesus who washed his

Rembrandt van Rijn (Colorized by Esther Hiʻilani Candari)

disciples' feet and was persuaded to stay and sup with importuning friends seems increasingly remote—roles now subsumed by a truer identity celebrated in art and hymns, along with anticipation of his glory-shrouded return.

In recent decades, prominent voices have worked to rekindle astonishment at the Incarnation as itself the news that Jesus was the *fullest* revelation of God. Kierkegaard makes this point emphatically in his reading of Philippians: "This form of a servant is not something put on like the king's plebian cloak, which just by flapping open would betray the king . . . —but it is his true form. For this is the boundlessness of true love, that in earnestness and in truth and not in jest it wills to be

Rembrandt van Rijn (Colorized by Esther Hiʻilani Candari)

the equal of the beloved. . . . The presence of the god himself in human form—indeed in the lowly form of a servant—is precisely the teaching."[6]

What teaching? That God's being and power and influence are a function of love, the love of a God who heals, sacrifices, and queries his friends earnestly if they love him in response. The teaching that absolute but effable love, acted out in concrete ways from Bethlehem to Calvary, as well as at the shore of Galilee and on the road to Emmaus, is the essence of God and his kingdom. No other power or dominion is worthy of God or his disciples. Christ's incarnation was not strategic or instrumental. It was lived solidarity with his people and the fullest revelation of God the Father. Helen Oppenheimer has reminded us of this aspect of *at one ment,* by taking seriously the word's etymology: "For God nonetheless to have the right to say, 'behold, it is very good,' God had to experience at first hand the sufferings of mortal creatures. . . . Could any promised heaven justify what creatures have to undergo? Unless the creator is Incarnate in this world, and not only tells us it is worthwhile but finds it worthwhile alongside us."[7] ✻

1. Sallie McFague, *Models of God: Theology for an Ecological, Nuclear Age* (Philadelphia: Fortress Press, 1987), 55.

2. "The theologians of the early church were all subordinationists." Charles Freeman, *A New History of Early Christianity* (New Haven: Yale University Press, 2009), 239.

3. Mathetes, *Ante-Nicene Fathers Vol. I* (Grand Rapids, MI: Christian Classics Ethereal Library, 1885), 44.

4. George C. Berthold, trans., *Maximus Confessor: Selected Writings* (New York: Paulist Press, 1985), 102.

5. "The ancient church was ignorant of the kenotic theory, according to which the Word divests himself of certain attributes when he descends to our estate." Mark Edwards, *Catholicity and Heresy in the Early Church* (Farnham, UK: Ashgate, 2009), 151.

6. Søren Kierkegaard, *Philosophical Fragments* (Princeton: Princeton University Press, 1985), 31–32, 55–56.

7. Helen Oppenheimer, *Making Good: Creation, Tragedy and Hope* (London: SCM Press, 2001), 17.

PSALM

KATHRYN
KNIGHT
SONNTAG

No more
August thunder—seasons
no longer
discern themselves. Monarchs
                              shift
latitude.

My eyes   catch
the strangeness—   smoke instead
of lightning   yellowing
my body. Light

enters dark   enters light   enter
seers eating crumbs off
ancient tables.   Hear
the rustle
of garments—   somewhere

in the deep
silences,   fabric
of the universe
reweaves   itself under
the weight of our undoing—

if we dream what remains   undreamed,
begin again,   will you cover us

in eyes ...

      stretch our   *future*
out before, alate
and apterous   spacious enough

to see.

THE ANGEL'S RIGHT HAND

**JOHN
ROSENBERG**

*One feels at moments as if one
could with a touch convey a vision.*
— W. B. Yeats

I

IN THE MIDDLE OF THE TWELFTH century in the middle of nowhere, John the Hermit built a church. He dedicated his efforts to St. Nicholas (yes, *that* St. Nick) and to the needs of pilgrims crossing Spain's isolated Oca Mountains on their way to Compostela. On the north side of the church to the left of the altar, a singular capital presides over a common column; it enjoys a degree of notoriety unexpected for this desolate place because the fading sun strikes the capital's western face—depicting the Annunciation—each equinox at five o'clock. The first time I encountered the capital, I did not see it, not really: I was limp from the climb up the Oca Mountains and unprepared for annunciations of any kind. Three years later (after the COVID interregnum) I was back, and what I saw and *felt* that day changed my life.

The Annunciation of the Church of St. Nicholas is lovely, but it was not that scene that moved me, touched me; it was the subsequent scene in the narrative: the Nativity. On the right a woman stands at the head of Mary's bed. Her left arm reaches forward and adjusts the cushion

Sarah Hawkes

Sarah Hawkes

that supports Mary's back and head; the right arm reaches around Mary's back and tugs at the cushion from the other side. She is a midwife. Mary occupies the lower half of the central scene. She semi-reclines; her right arm extends over her lap and holds in place a delicately carved blanket, its eight folds worked in the style of classical drapery. She supports her head with her left hand. Three vessels (lamps?) hang from a shelf above the bed. To the left shines the star of Bethlehem.

Under the star two cows nuzzle the child, who dozes in a woven basket; the animals attend to the swaddling, grasping the blanket with their teeth and tightening it. To their left an angel gestures. The messenger's bare feet protrude beneath the manger-basket; her left hand touches the baby's feet, the index finger points toward the child, drawing our attention to him. The angel bends at the waist to her right and hovers over Joseph, right hand on Joseph's head. The angel's

smile projects the peace proclaimed to shepherds on another face of the capital. Joseph is seated; he leans on a tau-shaped staff and wearily rests his right cheek in his right hand. Joseph is old, his beard patriarchal. He sleeps. The slumbering Joseph—common in medieval Nativity scenes—confuses some observers. Why is Joseph sleeping through the most transcendent moment in Christian history—the moment of incarnation? Cannot he watch with the baby one hour? A mere moment of reflection calls to mind that in the first two chapters of Matthew's Gospel, Joseph dreams, often. Through dreams he is instructed about his part in the unfolding Christian narrative: Joseph must take the pregnant Mary as his wife; he is warned to flee to Egypt to escape Herod's violence; a third dream instructs Joseph to return to the "land of Israel"; in the final dream Joseph learns he is to take his family to Nazareth. Joseph's closed eyes and the angel's right hand are coded to recall these revelatory dreams. But the postures also suggest blessing, a blessing that perhaps Mary strains to hear by cupping her left hand around her ear.

II

The western world's ocularcentrism is well documented. Light, vision, knowledge, and wisdom are nearly exclusively associated with the visual sense; the metaphor of the "mind's eye" is such a familiar descriptor of imagination that we don't even recognize its metaphoric quality. However, during the last century we rediscovered, or at least reappreciated, synesthesia: the interrelation of the senses. It is that interrelation that, informed by my interest in the methods of *lectio divina*, allowed me to experience—fully—the eight-hundred-year-old carvings at St. Nicholas. The animals smell and taste; Mary and Joseph hear; the star and the lamps cast light that reveals contours. But it is the tactile sense of the sculpture that *grabbed* me, that *caught* my attention, that *touched* me. The midwife touches Mary; Mary feels the texture and warmth of the blanket. The angel touches the infant. The angel rests her *hand, forearm, and head* on Joseph's head, an expression of intimacy more eloquent and reassuring, perhaps, than the words whispered in Joseph's ear, which, naturally, are inaudible to us.

Aristotle taught that touch was the first sense developed and the only one required for life itself.[1] Harry Harlow and then Ashley Montagu demonstrated that touch stimulates human thriving.[2] The affective power of touch is apparent from the words we use to describe emotions: we are deeply *touched*; we *feel* happy or sad or unwell. *Tact* is required to navigate tricky interpersonal relations, and often defined using the word adroitness, which is fitting, since *adroit* derives from the French word for right hand, presumably the same hand used to *handle* difficult situations, and the same hand the angel uses to bless Joseph. Dacher Keltner notes that touch is "our fundamental language of social connection,"[3] and Pablo Maurette explains that touch constitutes the "last line of defense between the outside world and our interiority."[4] Perhaps that is why invasive touching

wounds deeply, like the very public and entirely unwanted kiss the head of the Spanish soccer federation planted on one of the winning players in last year's Women's World Cup.

Christ healed the wounded by touching them, or by allowing others to touch him. Except on Easter morning. In one particularly beautiful (and unsettling) depiction of the *noli me tangere* ("touch me not") scene, an ivory carved a few decades before the Nativity capital (in a city a few hours west of St. Nicholas), the Magdalene takes several steps toward Christ, hands reaching out to embrace. The closing parenthesis of Christ's body captures his retreat, curving away from Mary, while his right hand points at her head and his left hand points to her extended right hand. Christ's posture would be out of character if it were associated with a scene of healing—what if this were the scene with lepers? Centuries of tradition have surrendered to new translations that renew this sacred scene. These renderings of the original Greek do not prohibit touching, only a particular kind of touching: "stop clinging to me" (NASB), "do not cling to me" (ESV), "do not hold on to me" (NIV), "do not hold me back."[5] These translations assume not just a touch, but an embrace, and suggest lingering contact, perhaps one that required interruption given Christ's busy Sunday morning schedule. The point is that the most famous denial of touch in the Christian tradition was anything but.

III

Bernard of Clairvaux shared the twelfth century with John the Hermit. He was a mystic, a monk, an abbot, the founder of the Knights Templar and a major figure in the rise of the Cistercian order—highly influential along the Camino de Santiago. And he wrote about the theology of touch. Gordon Rudy notes that St. Bernard understood that grace was "immediate and reciprocal," just like touch. He adds that

> Bernard of Clairvaux suggested that touch can grasp spiritual truths that are inaccessible to the more superficial sense of sight. While God cannot be perceived by sight,

"faith reaches the unreachable, catches the unknown, grasps what cannot be measured, . . . takes hold of the uttermost, and in a way encompasses even eternity itself in its broad breast."

St. Bernard writes, "The soul affected perfectly by [holy fear and holy love] comprehends as with two arms, and *embraces*, binds and holds, and says, 'I *held him* and I will not let him go,'" and later, "To seize or grasp is not to know but to 'experience.' To be experienced is to be influenced or moved by God, to embrace and hold interiorly" (emphasis added).[6]

Bernard's theological musings were autobiographical. In the widely read *Flos Sanctorum* published in Spanish in 1599, we find an account of one of Bernard's visions: "Una vez estando llorando delante de un Crucifixo, el mismo Crucifixo extendió el brazo, y se le echó encima, abraxándole, y acariciándole con singular favor" (On one occasion while weeping before a Crucifix, the Crucifix itself extended its arm, reached out to him, embracing him and caressing him with singular favor).[7] Francisco Ribalta portrayed this scene with exceptional psychological insight and technical mastery in a painting completed between 1625 and 1627, now hanging in the Prado. This is a mystical "deposition" captured *in medias res*. Christ's feet remain anchored to the cross by a single nail, blood still dripping from the wound. His hands, however, are free, and reach down to embrace the ecstatic saint. When I view the painting, I can't decide if Christ is descending to meet the saint, or if he is pulling St. Bernard up to him, making this painting an "ascent to the cross." However we read it, the painting portrays touch as a gesture of divine acceptance; Christ's right arm extends around Bernard's left shoulder, his left arm reaches under Bernard's limp right arm and raises it up.

IV

A different Bernard, Father Bernardo García Pintado, is a monk at the abbey of Santo Domingo de Silos, located a short drive from the church of St. Nicholas. He will turn ninety this year. Post-COVID

he uses a walker to move around the monastery, his body a comma, morphing into a compact graphism after a lifetime of writing, reading, and prayer. He has a wry and mischievous sense of humor and a broad smile that frames a joyful chuckle. He is my spiritual mentor and friend.

The day I experienced the capital at St. Nicholas, I drove to Silos to spend an afternoon with Bernardo. We talked of personal things, about his monastic vocation and ministry and about my quest to experience the love of God more fully. I explained to him that Christian doctrine makes sense to me: it appeals to my rational sense; it is beautiful in ways that are difficult for me to put in words; it appeals to my aesthetic sense. But I have struggled to *feel* the love of God, largely I suspect because I do not feel lovable. A great mystery of my life is experiencing copious amounts of love from every side while sensing that nothing inside me merits that affection. How does one break through this (surely self-imposed) barrier, I asked. I recounted my visit earlier that day to St. Nicholas and my experience with the Nativity capital, how that experience amplified my appreciation for the sense of touch. Bernardo acknowledged the power of touch, and then leaned forward and placed his hand a centimeter from my cheek. "¿Lo notas?" he asked. "One can sense the emanations of touch without actually being touched." We remained in that odd posture until he pulled himself to his feet, shuffled toward me, placed his hands on my head, like the angel to Joseph, and with that touch blessed me. I don't recall the words he spoke; I am not even sure I heard them. The touch, however, was redemptive, fulfilling the encircling promised in the Book of Mormon: "encircled in the robes of his righteousness" (2 Nephi 4:33); "encircled eternally in the arms of his love" (2 Nephi 1:15); "encircled in the arms of safety" (Alma 34:16). That afternoon I knew as I was known.

Following Vespers I greeted another friend, Father Angel Abarca, and he invited me to share the eleventh-century cloister with him. It was that magical time of day: the sun was settling on the horizon, casting well-defined shadows. The swallows squabbled when they swooped and ascended and dived again into the cloistered

Sarah Hawkes

garden; the fountain at the cloister's *axis mundi* flowed reverently—one had to attend to it to hear it. Angel, unaware of the experience I had just had with Bernardo, stopped in the middle of our stroll around the cloister and said he would like to give me a . . . blessing.

And then he offered another gift: the chance to spend time alone in the cloister. No tourists. No monks. Just the exquisite Romanesque carvings of Christ's life, and me. He left to attend to his duties, and I made multiple circuits around the cloister, pausing before each sculpture, letting my thoughts wander, pilgrimly. I stopped to look at a historiated capital on the west side—a Nativity scene. I knew it was there, but when it was crowded by the usual tourist throng, I had never been able to pause long enough to read carefully. Though weathered by exposure to the freezing winters, the capital retains shadows of original polychrome. The figures are easy to decipher: the Virgin and Elizabeth, Mary and the midwife, and the Holy Family fleeing to Egypt. Two slender columns support the double capital; the space between the columns is bridged by two figures: Joseph on the left, head bowed and resting on his left hand, sleeping, dreaming; and on the right, an angel, poised horizontally, his right hand gently touching Joseph's head. I thought, perhaps it is not words that heal, but touch.

Jacob wrestled all night with a man, an angel, or God, gripping, grasping, pulling, pushing until dawn. "Noli me tangere," his opponent demanded at sunrise, seeking to break free of Jacob's embrace. Jacob's reply: "I will not let you go until you bless me." On that day surrounded by saints, some carved, some flesh, none would let me go until they blessed me. And like Jacob, on that day I departed with the new identity of one who was touched and who discovered that he was worthy of love. ✻

1. Aristotle, *De Anima*, trans. Hugh Lawson-Tancred (New York: Penguin Classics, 1986), 220.

2. Harry F. Harlow, "The Nature of Love," *American Psychologist* 13 (1958): 676; Ashley Montagu, *Touching: The Human Significance of the Skin* (New York: Harper and Row, 1978), 1.

3. Quoted in Cynthia Gorney, "The Power of Touch," *National Geographic*, June 2022, 48.

4. Pablo Maurette, *The Forgotten Sense: Meditations on Touch* (Chicago: University of Chicago Press, 2018), 12.

5. Thomas A. Wayment, trans., *The New Testament: A Translation for Latter-day Saints* (Provo, UT: Religious Studies Center, Brigham Young University, 2019), 204.

6. Gordon Rudy, *Mystical Language of Sensation in the Later Middle Ages* (New York: Routledge, 2002), 57–59.

7. Pedro de Rivadeneyra, *Flos sanctorum* (Madrid: Luis Sánchez, 1599), 572.

THE BEAUTY OF HOLINESS

KRISTINE HAGLUND

WHEN I WAS ALMOST EIGHT, earnestly trying to do what was expected of a soon-to-be-baptized member of The Church of Jesus Christ of Latter-day Saints, I decided I needed to participate in the customary fast on the first Sunday of the month. Skipping breakfast before church was easy, but not eating lunch left me cranky by two or three in the afternoon. My long-suffering but exasperated mother responded to my whining by suggesting a few distracting activities, all of which I pronounced "dumb." She finally said, not hopefully, "Maybe you could read the scriptures. Maybe Psalms?" I liked the idea of Psalms—a beloved schoolteacher had given me a pocket-sized "Testament and Psalms," which I kept in my box of treasures but hadn't really read. I took it down to my favorite basement reading spot—a remnant of green carpet laid next to the woodstove, where the comforting warmth from the stove generally made up for the annoyance of the splinters of wood that worked their way into the carpet and thence occasionally into a reclining reader's elbows.

I dutifully read for a while, interrupted occasionally by impressively loud stomach grumblings, and had almost given up when I got to Psalm 29 and was arrested by the phrase "worship him in the beauty of holiness." I knew from Joseph Smith's story that sometimes a scripture could leap from the page and change the world, and I recognized this as my own Epistle of James moment, which would cleave my life into before and after. (This sounds very dramatic. I was a dramatic child. But it is also the truest way I know to tell the story.) I did not cry, not then. But I did go and get my violin and start practicing the most beautiful thing I knew, and I worked myself into tears with the little sighing grace notes in the third measure of the Brahms Waltz in Suzuki Book 2.

It is a strangely precise memory, perhaps because the details laid out the only nearly infallible mechanism for accessing the transcendent that I have discovered in my life: the recognition—often faint—of an idea, a "stroke of thought" that evokes a kind of longing that is not assuaged, but heightened and intensified by trying to capture the feeling in words or music. I know the details, because I have lived them, with slight variations of the carpet color and the text and the music involved, hundreds of times.

Curiously, I experienced that moment not as a revelation about God, but as a moment of *self*-revelation. That is, I was aware more or less instantly that this would be both method and content of my testimony. What I know, and nearly all I have been given to know, is the aching, joyous longing for the beauty of holiness. I don't really believe Keats's famous couplet: "Beauty is truth, truth beauty,—that is all / Ye know on earth, and all ye need to know."[1] There is plenty of truth in the world that is ugly, or harsh and bracing, and I have fallen for some beautiful lies. Nevertheless, the things I believe most deeply about God—the tiny list of things I am sure of—have come to me as traces of beauty tinged with a yearning something like homesickness. I am not convinced that beauty is always truth, but the entanglement of beauty and truth is, for me, a wellspring of joy.

The problem with this story is that it ought to be the backstory of a talented musician or composer or painter or sculptor, and I am none of those. I am a middling violinist with rusting skills, and a solid utility alto. It is also not a particularly promising origin story for someone who is going to be spiritually nurtured in the workaday, low church traditions of Latter-day Saint worship. My peculiar mode of access to the spiritual realm, combined with a notable lack of any evident artistic gifts, and the coincidence of being born into a cheerfully practical religious tradition that does not generally invest overmuch in artistic excellence in worship, is a recipe for restless frustration. I am saved by moments of unexpected grace and what at least one exhausted Primary teacher called "sheer cussedness."

I occasionally went back to the Psalms as I grew up, and I started to recognize the poetry in Isaiah and felt its tug. But there was easier poetry to be captivated by—Edna St. Vincent Millay's poems for young people, then her sonnets; my mother's beloved Emily Dickinson; George Herbert, whose "Easter Wings" inspired a few attempts at shape poems that even at fifteen I could see needed to be not merely discarded, but burned; Gerard Manley Hopkins's "Pied Beauty," which was (in what I am happy to call a miracle) a handout on the Sunday I graduated from Primary into Young Women. My father warned me sternly, after yet another assignment as youth speaker which I fulfilled mostly by reading e.e. cummings over the pulpit, that I should not get *all* my theology from poetry, to which I responded that Isaiah seemed to have been Jesus's major theological influence, so I didn't see what the problem was. (A prime example of the aforementioned cussedness.)

I went away to college and had a freshman year straight out of a college brochure or an overwrought nineteenth-century novel about the delights of the mind. I took courses in politics and literature, German lyric poetry, philosophy, and music. I sang in a choir that went to New York to perform in Carnegie Hall on my eighteenth birthday. And I sang in the chapel choir, discovering the possibilities for creating beautiful, reverent worship services with professional organists and conductors and auditioned singers. On Sundays, I would spend the morning in the majestic chapel in the middle of campus, feeling my heart leap at the first chords of the Old Hundredth and the simple psalm paraphrase of William Kethe:

> All people that on earth do dwell,
> Sing to the Lord with cheerful voice!
> Him serve with mirth, his praise forth tell;
> Come ye before him and rejoice.

A service typically included three or four hymns, plus choral prelude and postludes, an anthem, and a choral benediction or amen, often some service music or a communion anthem. Always there were responsive readings of Psalms.

My senior year, a new conductor, freshly arrived from England, decided to teach us

The entanglement of beauty and truth is, for me, a wellspring of joy.

Anglican chant. It is hard to describe how I felt in that first rehearsal figuring out how to read the tune at the top of the page and make the words fit with a series of instructions provided by a few simple symbols, mostly |, *, ·, and an occasional —. The first attempts were awkward, but after a few minutes, I felt like I was speaking my native language for the first time. I didn't have words for the sense of joyous homecoming. I had felt that way in a Latter-day Saint service only once, fleetingly, when I was very small, and a fine organist opened up all the very big stops for the pedal as we sang "Far, Far Away on Judea's Plains."

Maybe, I thought, that's to be expected. After all, it's hard to know what coming home feels like if you have never left. I tried not to notice that the way I felt singing Psalms in this ancient tradition seemed akin to what many people describe when they convert to The Church of Jesus Christ of Latter-day Saints.

It wasn't that I didn't have a testimony of my own church. I did. I had had a few powerful experiences I couldn't explain away, and I wanted to be faithful to the truths I had received in Latter-day Saint contexts. But what to do with the sweetness of this recognition that felt like homecoming?

I would like to say that I have figured it out, or that my conviction of the truth of The Church of Jesus Christ of Latter-day Saints overwhelms every uncertainty. But that isn't true. I struggle to make sense of how like a fish out of water I feel at church sometimes, and I have to work hard to figure out how to contribute meaningfully in a church where so many people seem to connect to God in a different way than I do. Have I missed my calling because I stayed in my religious home? What does it mean that the gifts that seem most precious to me are seldom wanted where I have promised to offer everything?

I have no answers to these questions, or to the most painful question of all—why was I given the gift of loving music, and not the gift I have always wanted most—to be good at singing the praises I hear so clearly in my heart? The years seem only to bring more questions.

But some of the questions are gracious—big enough to stretch my understanding and

> ## Making things beautiful is WORK, not the magical efflorescence of *talent* or *passion* or any of the flimsier things we sometimes call *art*.

make faith possible. One comes from a beloved Christmas carol, "In the Bleak Midwinter": What can I give him?

My chronic grief about not being a great musician makes me wonder earnestly about the disconnect between what I think God would like and what I can actually give. It occurs to me sometimes that *most* of what we bring to the altar is not nearly as valuable as we suppose. The difficulty of figuring out what the Lord wants from us is illustrated in Genesis by Cain's rejected sacrifice, articulated again in Samuel's insistence that "to obey is better than sacrifice," and the psalmist's recognition that "thou desirest not sacrifice; else would I give it: thou delightest not in burnt offering. The sacrifices of God are a broken spirit: a broken and a contrite heart, O God, thou wilt not despise." The Nephites are instructed that their "burnt offerings shall be done away, for I will accept none of your sacrifices and your burnt offerings." And just before the Saints at Kirtland are asked to give a tithe of money to build the temple, a new kind of sacrifice, they're reminded that "all among them who know their hearts are honest, and are broken, and their spirits contrite, and are willing to observe their covenants by sacrifice—*yea, every sacrifice which I, the Lord, shall command*—they are accepted of me."[1]

Perhaps we need to be told exactly what to sacrifice because we aren't very good at recognizing what is valuable. Maybe Paul's description of gifts within the body of Christ isn't just about other people's gifts that we wrongly think are less worthy than our own, but about our estimation of what it is we ourselves have to offer.

> Nay, much more those members of the body, which seem to be more feeble, are necessary:
> And those members of the body, which we think to be less honourable, upon these we bestow more abundant honour; and our uncomely parts have more abundant comeliness.
> For our comely parts have no need: but God hath tempered the body together, having given more abundant honour to that part which lacked.[2]

Maybe artistic gifts, like all the others, are useful for bringing us to the place where we can offer all that we really have to give—our brokenness, our need, our yearning to know and be known.

And this brings me to the biggest and most helpful question for me: What is beautiful? Or, in Gerard Manley Hopkins's lovelier formulation, "To what serves mortal beauty?" and "What do then? How meet beauty?"

A lot of debates about Christian aesthetics worry through these questions, starting from the premise that the beautiful is costly, in money or time or unequally distributed talents, and that those resources ought to be used for more practical kinds of discipleship. Other askers of these questions are troubled by the possibility that art will draw attention to itself and away from God. Latter-day Saints seem to be nervous about the arts on both counts, in ways that are clear more from our practice than our doctrine: choir practice is never going to take precedence over ward council, and maintaining the floor of the basketball court is usually a higher priority than tuning the pianos. The art that is part of our worship is not chosen by artists or trained critics, but by men with ecclesiastical authority. Their appraisal of what kinds of art and music are suitable for Latter-day Saint worship carries more weight than the considered judgment of people who spend all their lives thinking about what is beautiful or true; we are, institutionally, wary of people

J. Kirk Richards

who think that beauty could tell us something about God that authority cannot. I don't know any artists or musicians in the Church who don't chafe at these constraints.

And yet, on my more patient and charitable days, I am able at least to ask whether these constraints may tether us to what Hopkins calls "God's better beauty, grace." After all, the closest thing to an aesthetic theory for the Restoration presents itself in section 42 of the Doctrine and Covenants, in a passing reference to beautiful garments in Zion:

And again, thou shalt not be proud in thy heart; let all thy garments be plain, and their beauty the beauty of the work of thine own hands. . . .

Thou shalt not be idle; for he that is idle shall not eat the bread nor wear the garments of the laborer.

And whosoever among you are sick, and have not faith to be healed, but believe, shall be nourished with all tenderness, with herbs and mild food, and that not by the hand of an enemy. . . .

Thou shalt live together in love, insomuch that thou shalt weep for the loss of them that die.[3]

This is beauty not as aesthetic, but as *ethic*, part of the consecration of all human striving within a community committed to a tender regard for every member and for the labor that sustains bodies and souls. And while it might be read to

Worshiping God in the beauty of holiness is a different thing than worshiping beauty.

minimize the importance of beautiful things, and certainly is a warning against aesthetic snobbery, it also offers the possibility of sanctification for working to make things beautiful; it insists that skillful handwork can matter deeply in God's economy of time and effort, which makes me hopeful about choir rehearsals in Zion.

It begins to answer the question "what is beauty" in a more expansive way than our usual post-Enlightenment, post-Romantic theorizing. It situates the beautiful in the life of a community, insists that it is not only a matter of self-expression. It recognizes, in a way that we sometimes fail to attend to in other contexts, that making things beautiful is WORK, not the magical efflorescence of "talent" or "passion" or any of the flimsier things we sometimes call "art." And it allows for the possibility that the beautiful will exist right alongside the terrible—idleness and pride, illness and disease, even death. It is a human and earthbound beauty that God commends to us.

Here finally is the truth of it for me: God wants to tell us, all the time, that creation is good, that this world and all that is in it is beloved. The stirrings I felt as a child by the woodstove and with my squeaky little violin were real and true, but they were not meant to pull me towards transcendence so much as to push me towards love. Beauty is an index to the divine not because it lifts us out of the earth, but because it lets us see the ways we are part of it and lets us hear God whispering that "it is very good." God's love of the creation includes not only the rose, but the thorns and the dirt and the earthworms and even the aphids. What God calls beautiful is not only the expertly performed Bach prelude, but the toddler running to his nursery teacher with arms outstretched, a loaf of bread baked for the sacrament by one of the high priests, that one Sunbeam yelling every song in the Primary program, the surreptitious passing of tissues during testimony meeting, a stack of variously shaded and wrinkled hands laid together to give a blessing, the endless passing of signup sheets to help with moves, rides to Girls Camp, chapel cleaning, the sacrament of ham and potato casseroles after funerals. We build our part of Zion with wood and stone and mud, and then God promises to restore our wastelands and make our feeble gifts worthy of his habitation—he will, in Isaiah's words, lay our stones with fair colours, and lay our foundations with sapphires, make our windows of agates, our gates Salvation and our walls Praise.

None of this makes me stop going to Evensong services and choir concerts and loving them. It doesn't completely assuage the grief of not having enough time or talent to make the kind of music I long for. None of this is to say that I have become reconciled to bad music in our worship services, or that I don't believe God wants us to work more diligently at creating beauty. It is only to say that I am, ever so belatedly, beginning to understand that worshiping *God* in the beauty of holiness is a different thing than worshiping beauty, and that holiness is beautiful in both the poetry of the Psalms and in the homely prose of a dutiful life. Indeed, I may say that I follow the admonition of Zephaniah:

"Sing, O daughter of Zion; shout, O Israel; be glad and rejoice with all the heart, O daughter of Jerusalem.
The Lord hath taken away thy judgments, he hath cast out thine enemy: the king of Israel, even the Lord, is in the midst of thee: . . . Fear thou not. . . .
The Lord thy God in the midst of thee is mighty; he will save, he will rejoice over thee with joy; he will rest in his love, he will joy over thee with singing." [4] ✷

This essay will appear in a forthcoming volume of essays A Thoughtful Faith for the 21st Century, *edited by Philip L. Barlow and published by Faith Matters.*

1. Genesis 4:3–5; 1 Samuel 15:22; Psalm 51:16–17; Doctrine and Covenants 97:8.

2. 1 Corinthians 12:22–24.

3. Doctrine and Covenants 42:40, 42–43, 45.

4. Zephaniah 3:14–17.

Appearance of Christ

IVANKA DEMCHUK

HOW DO WE LIVE WITH THE PAST?

A Meditation on Nostalgias

JAMES GOLDBERG

WHEN THE WORLD SEEMS TO be falling apart around me, I think of Svetlana Boym.

Boym was a professor of literature, an artist, and a perceptive cultural critic. Born in Leningrad in 1959 to a family already disillusioned with the official national dream of a workers' paradise, she fled the Soviet Union at age nineteen. At the time, she thought she might never see her parents or childhood home again. But in the United States, she outlived the terms of her exile: in 1991, the Soviet system collapsed.

That same year, the Sistine Chapel reopened after a decade-long closure to care for Michelangelo's ceiling frescoes. Rather than merely working to head off decay, the Vatican had authorized a team of specialists to remove layers of ash and grime. Using a computer-aided technique to strip away intervening layers, the conservation team promised to bring back the brightness of the original colors. But not everyone was happy. A few art historians argued that the removals were going too far, erasing some of Michelangelo's own charcoal outlining and shadows. In the end, the cleaning wiped the pupils off a few figures' eyes.

On a trip back to Europe, Boym saw the finished product. Looking up at the ceiling, she missed the once-prominent crack in the paint between God and Adam. Beyond questions of whether the project had gotten Michelangelo's intentions right, she worried that the attempt to remake the frescoes as *they had been* was getting in the way of the masterpiece *they had become*. For her, a great artwork is much more than a good painting. Great art gathers associations over time; its history is part of its power. What computer models coded as ash and grime, Boym saw as traces from generations' worth of candles and incense. For her, the brightened color mattered less than a discarded aura of history.

How exactly are we expecting to be transported through time when we visit a historical place or work of art? As she considered the Sistine Chapel ceiling and other examples, Boym categorized approaches into two broad types. In *The Future of Nostalgia*, she uses the term *restorative nostalgia* to describe efforts to remake the present in the image of a real or imagined past. To do so, she noted, restorative projects have to settle on a pristine moment to be restored, as if setting the dial on a time machine—like the Sistine Chapel team choosing to transport viewers back to the moment the paint on the ceiling dried (even if that was before the pupils were drawn on). A disappointing present could be replaced, and erased, by that specific, desired layer of the past. Boym contrasted this with an approach she called *reflective nostalgia*. Reflective nostalgia, she wrote, was less about the return home than the longing for it. It involved a relationship with the past that embraced the cracks and decay, in which a viewer's goal was not to reach a given past but to reflect on time's passage. For Boym, the great virtue of the reflective mode was the flexibility it offered, allowing viewers to examine time without becoming locked into any given layer.

For Boym, these questions about nostalgia were not only about how we handle aging works of art. Looking at eastern Europe in the 1990s, she also wanted to know how societies would relate to their pasts. Some chose reflective routes. In Prague, for example, Boym visited a giant statue of a metronome, which had been commissioned to fill the empty pedestal of an old communist monument. But not everyone felt so playful. By the mid-1990s, as high expectations for the post-Soviet era gave way to upheaval and uncertainty, *Old Songs About the Most Important Things* made its way up Russian CD sales charts, and millions tuned into a TV show called *The Old Apartment*. Boym worried that the growing marketing power of the word *old* revealed a longing for "the good old days, when everyone was young, some time before the big change."[1] Though she knew that the good old days are usually a mirage, she also recognized that imagined pasts can have real consequences. If leaders decided to restore a lost Russia, what would they first have to try to wipe away?

In 2014, Boym was diagnosed with cancer. That same year, Russian troops slipped into Crimea and eastern Ukraine. She died the next year, having already foreseen how the way we approach an old painting might relate to the ways we wage war. Countries make poor canvases. Now I scroll through news about young men, often drafted against their will, who fight over the meaning of the past with tanks, drones, and artillery on muddy battlefields reminiscent of World

> # The great virtue of the reflective mode was the flexibility it offered, allowing viewers to examine tim⟨e⟩ without becoming locked into any given layer.

War I. A thousand miles farther south, Israelis and Palestinians are caught between the mutually exclusive visions of Hamas, which is determined to restore Muslim sovereignty from the River Jordan to the Mediterranean Sea, and figures like Bezalel Smotrich, whose ambitions to expand Israeli territory are driven by ideas about the past rather than realistic assessments of the present.

Elsewhere, too, people have been caught by the claims of imagined pasts. As voters find the present lacking, I read about a worldwide wave of nationalist political parties who promise that they alone can vanquish pain and turn back time. In my neighborhood, I walk past flags that say *Make America Great Again*. With some vital bonding agent losing strength, the world seems to be falling apart around me.

And I think of Svetlana Boym.

I live in a global twenty-first century. But I live as a Latter-day Saint.

How do we relate to our past? It's hard to say. In Nauvoo, sites take a restorative approach. Instead of a monument to the scattered stones of the temple, I can visit whole blocks set to mimic the city at its height. The houses are furnished; the patterns in the wallpaper are uniformly taken from the early 1840s; the blacksmith shop is open for business. At the Daughters of Utah Pioneers Museum in Salt Lake, I get a very different experience—one more consistent with Boym's descriptions of reflective nostalgia. Somewhere between the case filled with bits of pioneer barbed wire and the turn-of-the-century fire truck tucked into the basement, there's a graying piece of sacrament bread saved from the Salt Lake Temple's dedication. Rather than transporting me to the past, these exhibits remind me that I'm standing in the present, looking from a distance over a lost world of fruit dolls and hair wreaths. In other places, utilitarian concerns prevail over either mode of nostalgia. In our recent reconstruction of the Salt Lake Temple, for example, we just tore out the original murals and tucked the pieces away.

But the past doesn't always stay in storage. The past few decades have had their own upheavals and uncertainties for Latter-day Saints. In the late twentieth century, Church growth and a family-centered culture were important pillars of our collective identity. Prominent statistical differences in the early twenty-first century include lower conversion rates, activity rates, marriage rates, and birth rates. Accompanying these measurable differences is a general sense of weight, an intuition that the Church is somehow carrying more baggage than it once did. In an early *Wayfare* piece, Joseph Spencer observed that it's become far more complicated to live in American society as a Latter-day Saint since the end of the 1990s. He mentions changes like "increased political divisiveness, the internet-enabled expansion of information, new forms of identity politics, the rise of social media, and the impact of a global pandemic," as well as a shrinking sense that there's much outside the economic and social systems we now spend our time debating.[2]

Whatever larger social forces and internal dynamics are at work, it's easy to see how a Latter-day Saint today might long for a different

Matthew Picton

time. A missionary in a secularizing society might read wistfully about mass conversions in nineteenth-century England. A Primary president might wish for a time when the average member spent more attention on the ward, and it was less of a challenge to fill callings. A person who walks on eggshells with a loved one over differences in faith might wish for an alternate reality where the shared rhythms of religious life can still be taken for granted. We may be looking back with rose-colored glasses, but of course we look back.

And when we look back, we often want to put things back the way we think they were. This impulse toward a restorative nostalgia for our recent history can take many forms. I often hear people speak wistfully, for example, about an idealized pre-Correlation past, a time when the Church was less institutional and impersonal. Like the Sistine Chapel ceiling's aggressive conservators, some dream of wiping away the layers of bureaucracy that accumulate with age to bring back a lost communal vibrance. Unfortunately, an overzealous opposition to bureaucracy can make it hard to acknowledge the humanity of individual bureaucrats (and in the Church, many of us end up enlisted in that category at one time or another). Rather than seeing an organization president, a bishop, or a prophet as a rounded human wrestling with genuine complexity, a lens of restorative nostalgia can make them look like obstacles, then enemies. It turns out to be shockingly easy to demonize others while speaking for unrestrained fellowship and love.

Other Saints really miss manuals from thirty years ago. People in this group long for days just before the internet, when Church publications could offer simpler, more streamlined shared narratives. In search of a time before they were expected to think about Joseph Smith's use of seer stones or wrestle with his introduction of plural marriage, a growing minority are now embracing conspiracy theories about the Church's early history—such as that Joseph never introduced polygamy, or that Brigham Young orchestrated Joseph Smith's assassination. Friends of mine who study Nauvoo history have been baffled by these theories' remarkable persistence in the face of strong historical evidence. But not all problems with history can be solved by the methods of professional historians. How persuasive can we expect 1840s documents to be if someone's real problem is that they don't like the 2000s?

Still other Saints seem to yearn, on some level, for the apparent moral clarity of the Cold War years, when their political and religious convictions could be merged into a shared critique of one clear enemy. In some quarters, patriotism and devotion are urgently searching for an enemy to rally against. The irony is that these Saints' and patriots' thirst for comforting extremes often leads to conflict with the moderate forces in Church and government. In the most acute cases, the longing for a past defined by national and religious loyalty turns people aggressively against nation and religion. (How many anti-government words have been uttered under the banner of the US flag? How many heresies, holding a Bible?)

The hope for some kind of connection with the past is deeply human. It may well run as deep as hunger or sexual desire. But hunger and desire can easily damage individuals and relationships if they are not channeled in an effective way. It matters a great deal how we think about what we want.

I sympathize with Saints who feel unmoored. I, too, feel the terror of these currents we are passing through. The siren song of return to a safer past calls out to us—but if we listen too long to that melody, the story always seems to end with someone dashed against the rocks.

Just over a decade ago, when I first encountered Svetlana Boym's work, I didn't respond so viscerally to her warnings about nostalgia's dangers. Instead, her work piqued my intellectual curiosity. I was struck by the fact that her category of *restorative nostalgia* shared a key term with my belief in a *restored gospel*. Was that only a coincidence? Or was Latter-day Saint use of the term *restore* a sign of the nostalgia built into our religious view of time?

Boym's work pushed me to more deeply consider Joseph Smith's work. I thought about his aesthetics, about the particular kind of temporal logic that guided him. Clearly, he was a prophet preoccupied with the past. But what did Joseph Smith want from it?

To understand the flavors of Joseph Smith's nostalgia for the religious past, it may be helpful to begin with a point of comparison. Many other Christian leaders have been interested in the lost practices of Jesus's earliest followers. Alexander Campbell, a Christian primitivist preacher and publisher active in nineteenth-century Ohio who was a mentor to Sidney Rigdon, offers a fairly direct point of reference for considering Joseph Smith's work.

Deeply influenced by Enlightenment thinkers, Campbell believed in using common-sense rationalism to strip away historical accretions until he and his followers reached bedrock biblical truths. From that assumption, he reasoned that all the world's Christian denominations could easily be united into one body if they would only return to a past moment of consensus before any splintering took place.

In search of that moment, Campbell was selective about which parts of scripture he considered authoritative. In his writings, he dismissed the Old Testament as an artifact of fulfilled Mosaic law with no relevance to Christians' salvation. He likewise cordoned off the miracles in the New Testament, framing them as signs to confirm the truth of the gospel, supplanted after the time of the apostles by the recorded witness of scripture itself. To reclaim the Bible, Campbell was quite willing to flatten it. Boym's ideas about restorative nostalgia can help us explain these boundaries to Campbell's biblical consciousness. Like other restorative projects, Campbell's quest was necessarily aimed at a specific and static moment in time. In his case, the moment of lost Christian unity could be reclaimed exactly at the seam where the Bible ends and subsequent history begins.

Alexander Campbell and Joseph Smith agreed on many points. Both rejected infant baptism, advocated an organizational structure inspired by the New Testament church, and prioritized principles like faith, repentance, and baptism. But their approaches to the past could hardly be more different.

While Campbell attempted to recover a pristine past through biblical analysis, Joseph Smith was publishing the Book of Mormon as an ancient American volume of scripture, describing multiple interactions with angels, and calling for the scattered house of Israel to gather in Ohio and Missouri. Rather than attempting to recover an obscured past by trimming the present down to its image, Joseph Smith was interested in expanding the present by feasting on an eclectic mix of genuinely lost pasts. Instead of singling out a static moment to restore, Joseph channeled multiple moments through mystical interaction or embodied, collective reenactment. The restored gospel arrived, in other words, as an ongoing recasting of many dynamic moments in covenant history.

This is deeply strange stuff. If Alexander Campbell's approach was like scraping unwanted layers off the ceiling of the Sistine Chapel, Joseph Smith's was more like restoring the chapel ceiling by painting a wild new work in the same spirit across the chapel floor.

One striking feature of Joseph Smith's mode of bridging past and present is its radical embrace of simultaneity. The revelations he received draw liberally on Old and New Testaments, mixing the images of the house of Israel and the primitive Church. He was energized by thoughts of ancient Americans and ancient Egyptians. In the revelations and his teachings, Independence, Missouri, is many things. It is the site for a New Jerusalem, intended to coexist with rather than supplant the old holy city. It is a promised land on the border of Gentile and Lamanite, an intersection full of forgotten pasts and promises. It is an echo and twin of Enoch's Zion, a copy which will someday meet and merge with the original in a moment of mutual culmination. It is the Garden of Eden—the beginning of the world—at the same time it is a site where Christ will come suddenly to his temple at the world's end.

To lay the cornerstone for a temple half a world away from the ruins of the still-revered Jerusalem original hardly feels like Boym's restorative nostalgia, where one past conquers another.

Matthew Picton

But to literally lay a cornerstone for a temple at all feels different than Boym's category of reflective nostalgia, which calls attention to the passage of time and the inevitability of loss.

In Missouri, arguably, the early community of Saints ran up against waves of hostile local restorative nostalgia. Branded as a threat to the Way It Used To Be, they were driven from their homes. For helping us understand the Saints' emerging approach to nostalgia, the expulsion from the original site of Zion is instructive. What role would Independence, Missouri, play in the Latter-day Saint imagination after it was lost?

The dream of return, and concrete efforts to restore the Saints to their promised lands, are an important theme in the early 1830s. But alongside those efforts, a fascinating development unfolds. Within a few years of expulsion from their Eden in Independence, revelations to Joseph Smith designate some of the unwanted upper Missouri lands they had come to occupy as Adam-ondi-Ahman, the place where Adam and Eve built an altar after leaving the Garden. In an alchemy of longing, the place of exile becomes a sacred space.

Roughly the same happens in Nauvoo, which is named for the particular saving beauty referenced in Isaiah 52:7. And then again with places like Mount Pisgah on the pioneer trail, or in Utah with its salt sea, Jordan River, and Zion in the mountaintops. Latter-day Saints can still weep

for their promised land in Missouri, but there is no need to fight for it. Someday, the Lord will fight their battles. In the meantime, the sense of promise seems to follow them, flow through them, wherever they go.

What could we call this mode of nostalgia? Both Boym's categories begin from an assumption of an unmoored present looking toward the past for either a fixed anchor or an orienting landmark. But for Joseph Smith, the past can also move. Under the right supplications, the past responds and engages in open conversation with the present. In personal and shared supernatural experiences, Joseph and others conversed with angels—who they understood not as separate heavenly beings, but as resurrected figures from human history who could bring old tools to the work of a new epoch. In Doctrine and Covenants 130, Joseph Smith taught that angels access past, present, and future, which exist continually before the Lord. In contexts like the temple endowment, Saints could likewise bridge time, bringing ancestors' time and sacred history into conversation with the present.

I call this mode of engagement *mystical recall*. *Recall* because it involves bridging the distance between past and present by summoning the past. *Mystical* in reference to the Greek term *mystes*—meaning an initiate who received knowledge through a sacred drama—because the past has to be met, has to be given room to listen and act, for such summoning to work.

The technique is not unique to ancient mystery rites or to Mormonism. At a Passover seder table, Jews are slaves in Egypt. This is true every year and in any place. An observer might say that this image is only a metaphor to link the speaker to themes of oppression and deliverance, and that there's a vital distinction between the real table and symbolic Egypt. But I don't read the haggadah text that way any more than a Catholic simply eats a wafer or drinks wine during the Eucharist.

To me, these instances of religious language operate by power of their animating recall. In such moments of sacred drama, time collapses. The past and present become equally real and equally suggestive of a deeper reality. During the Latter-day Saint temple endowment, eras and identities coexist. I am James and my wife is Nicole; I am Adam and she is Eve.

In Latter-day Saint thought, this logic of mystical recall extends beyond ritual. Our worldview is woven out of living pasts, enchanted presents, and promising futures. Consider the concept of Zion. For us, Zion is a Jerusalem hill, but it is not only a Jerusalem hill. When we called it to Independence, it both came and remained in Jerusalem. When we called it to Deseret, it also remained in Independence. We are perpetually *building* Zion in our wards while also occasionally *experiencing* Zion in our wards at the same time Zion *waits for us* in past sites and a future city.

In the face of upheaval, we don't actually need to turn back the clock. Latter-day Saints' most successful method for moving on from periods of conflict and loss, of victimization and victimizing, has been to bring the past forward. That power remains in our reach.

Consider the example of the refugee crisis of 2015–2016. In that year, events like the Syrian civil war drove millions of people from their homes. In many European countries and the United States, the prospect of rapid population exchange led to a spike in support for aggressive nationalist groups. These groups played to fears about change and promised to put things back the way they used to be. But that's not at all the language and action that came from the Church.

Under Linda Burton's direction, the Relief Society called on the Saints to aid refugees. In that effort, Church leaders enlisted our collective memory. President Burton's April 2016 general conference address invoked Emma Smith's teachings to the Nauvoo Relief Society and quoted from Lucy Meserve Smith's accounts of the 1856 handcart rescue. Burton worked to turn her listeners' hearts, linking the contemporary spike in refugee needs into a genealogy of those extraordinary occasions.[3]

In his address, Elder Patrick Kearon worked to spiritually link Latter-day Saints to refugees through the shared dramas they had enacted. "As a people, we don't have to look back far in our history to reflect on times when we were refugees," Elder Kearon said. "Their story *is* our story." Far from presenting the past as a safe alternative to the challenges of mass migration, he summoned the past to explicitly call on modern Saints to rise to the challenge. "Let us come out from our safe places and share with them, from our abundance, *hope* for a brighter future, *faith* in God and in our fellowman, and *love* that sees beyond cultural and ideological differences to the glorious truth that we are all children of our Heavenly Father."[4]

Stirred by the spirit of mystical recall, my desire to live in easier times falls away. If we feel alone in this moment, we can cry out for Moroni. If we are lost in the wilderness, we can make it Adam-ondi-Ahman. We can live in the present and lift where we stand by summoning pasts to sustain us. God, grant us the hour's challenge. May it help us to reach deep. ✸

1. Svetlana Boym, *The Future of Nostalgia* (New York: Basic Books, 2001), 65.

2. Joseph M. Spencer, "Faith in the 21st Century," *Wayfare*, Winter 2022, 33–38.

3. Linda K. Burton, "I Was a Stranger," *Ensign*, May 2016, 13–15.

4. Patrick Kearon, "Refuge from the Storm," *Ensign*, May 2016, 111–14. Emphases in original.

NKATSENKWAN (GROUNDNUT STEW)

ALIXA
BROBBEY

Your father's love language is ignoring
your protests while he piles on more
and more rice. Your plate turns volcanic,

spewing stew sopping with palm oil.
The spices stain your thumbs, melting
your tongue numb. He calls you

skeleton, scoops up another smoking
serving. While you stuff yourself,
he remembers his own father, slurping
soup that singed his nostrils.

He remembers watching the shared bowl
pass from father to mother to oldest
brother until finally
landing lukewarm in his lap.

You lap up the last dregs, loosen
your belt. Remind yourself
this is the way he knows to love
you best, so tight you could collapse
into yourself.

OVERFLOWING WITH FAMILY

AMY
HARRIS

DO YOU HAVE A FAMILY? THE QUES-tion came over the phone from the stake family history coordinator. I had signed up to be a FamilySearch indexer, and she called to welcome me to the team and get to know me. Though "family" is a capacious category, I knew she was really asking two very narrow, specific questions: *Do you have a husband?* and *Do you have children?* Despite knowing that this kind, helpful, and sensitive woman was asking about my marital and maternal status, I decided not to tell her I had no husband or children, but to tell her the full truth, the full answer.

"Yes!" I answered, "I have a family." I then proceeded to rattle off details about my parents, eight siblings, four siblings-in-law, twelve nieces and nephews, two nieces-in-law, and the imminent arrival of my first great-nephew. A short but awkward pause followed. She had not expected my answer and wasn't quite sure of her footing. I don't recall which of us spoke first, but we pivoted and moved on in the conversation. She should feel lucky I didn't also mention my 110 first cousins or how I had inherited two centuries' tradition of childless aunts being adored by their families. And considering that not only am I a historian and genealogist, but also I had just volunteered to help with the stake's family history work, she's really lucky I didn't start spouting stories about my ancestors and how connected I feel to them.

Asking if someone has a family, a common question in most church settings, is a sensitive way people ask about spouses and children without making widowed or divorced people and childless couples divulge what could be painful details of their lives. And at that level, I appreciate it. But it also causes a little itch at the back of my mind because even the sensitive version of the question (instead of the blunt questions, *Are you a wife? Are you a mother?*) carries implied limitations that obscure my own family life.

I'm sure this stake worker doesn't remember our conversation, but I remember it with pride. I was glad she asked if I had a family and not if I had a husband, because answering the latter question ends with "no" (which doesn't bother me, but always seems to make my questioners uncomfortable). And, disturbingly, that answer is often followed with "So, it's just you, then" or "So, you're on your own then." No, it's not just me. No, despite living alone, I am most decidedly not on my own. But in the moment of these interactions, I'm not always prepared to list all the ways that I'm as far away from being on my own as one could practically get. So I was pleased with myself that in this instance I jumped on the chance to describe my family in all its glory, even if it was not the expected answer.

I live a life of plenty. I didn't earn it, and I don't deserve it, but I'm profoundly grateful for the fact that, particularly in family relationships, I've always enjoyed magnificent abundance. As the youngest of a large family and as a child of parents who also came from large families, the sheer number of my close relatives is staggering. Since that conversation with the stake family history specialist years ago, five additional nieces-in-law, a nephew-in-law, and twenty-four great nieces and nephews have joined my already bountiful family. I'm literally awash in a sea of relations. But my family isn't just quantity.

The quality of my family relationships consistently delights and amazes me. My sense of a place in the world and my hopes for the future are so intertwined with how I think about my family that I cannot separate myself from them. Being the youngest means I joined a family already in progress, and I have virtually no memories of young childhood that do not involve my parents and siblings. The ensuing decades have taken those childhood interactions and built on them until I feel continually buttressed and grounded by their presence in my life. I stride out into the

Laura Erekson

world with family streaming behind me like a cape and powering before me like a shield. They are the cup that consistently runneth over, the blessings showering from the windows of heaven I cannot contain, the dews of Carmel distilling upon me, and the human manifestation of the love of God, like the blossoms of a cherry tree, shedding itself abroad in my heart.[1]

That family reality, those living, breathing people who belong to me and I to them, color everything: how I understand discipleship and baptismal covenants, my deep well of appreciation for ancestors, my convictions about the power that binds us and all of humanity together and to our Heavenly Parents. It shapes my work, my conversations, my friendships, my service, my free time. And my faith consistently reminds me that my relationships with them matter for the long haul.

And yet, often all of my familial richness and abundances are not acknowledged at church. I can't determine exactly where the expectation comes from, but as a single and childless woman in a church that is so focused on marriage and child-rearing, I often feel as if I'm meant to check my existing and abundant family at the church door. Sometimes I feel that, because I don't have a spouse or children, I should not consider myself blessed, or consider myself as having a family. A husband or children would be cause for rejoicing, or at least recognition, but other relationships—sisters, brothers, aunts, and uncles—are rarely considered as important enough to be celebrated at church.

Being a sister is the cornerstone of my identity, both socially and spiritually. My entire life I've experienced a little thrill, a little frisson of excitement when one of my siblings introduces me to someone and says, "This is my sister." That sentence and the powerful sense of belonging it brings delights me every time I hear it. Being a sister has been just a fact of life. I always appreciated it, and that appreciation has grown over time, despite limited discussions at church of siblings' lifelong importance. Primary lessons in my childhood often discussed loving and getting along with siblings, but adult church curriculum focused only on obtaining and maintaining couplehood, followed by parenthood.

For my siblings, I was the doted-upon youngest, the one they named via democratic election, but they never treated me like the baby or the family mascot. Instead, my siblings just incorporated me into their existing patterns. They took me to movies and on hikes; they let me join road trips while I was still a preschooler; they passed along their teenage and young-adult wisdom; they taught me about football and etiquette, about love, loss, and death. I was there when they left on missions, when they moved into college dorms, when they played sports, and when they were in hospital beds. And I was there when they eventually made their way back for reunions or Thanksgiving dinners.

As I aged, I reciprocated more and more, and in some ways I caught up with them. The differences in our ages telescoped down until they were meaningless. I now ask for their advice and give my own in return. We stand together in temple prayer circles. We reminisce about family reunions and childhood homes. We combine resources when buying Christmas gifts for our parents and wedding and baby gifts for our nieces and nephews. We rally and mobilize in times of crisis, illness, and grief. Losing our parents was a communal experience, the sharp edges of grief made smoother and more bearable because the experience was shared.

I became an aunt a month before my twelfth birthday. I distinctly remember staring with my sister through the hospital nursery's window at our new, tiny, Yoda-looking nephew. He was followed in succession by eleven additional, slightly less Yoda-looking nieces and nephews. So, by the time I was twenty-seven, just as most of my friends were becoming parents, I had spent more than half my life as an aunt. I played with my nieces and nephews, watched over them, joked with them, read with them, and talked to them about sports and literature and faith. They visited me when I lived far away for graduate school, and I got to know them when I circulated among their parents' households for holidays. I sent birthday cards; they sent drawings, photographs, and postcards. I attended blessings and baptisms; they greeted me with posters and hugs when I returned from my mission. For me, being an aunt was just part of what it meant to have a family. Even now as those nieces and nephews have married and have children of their own, my relationship with them and their spouses grows in depth and meaning. And the feelings of protection and love I have for *their* children are fierce and powerful.

Being a sister and an aunt are some of the most fulfilling and meaningful relationships of my life, relationships that become even more fulfilling and meaningful when I appreciate them for what they are, instead of trying to make them a phase I will outgrow once I marry or have children, or "settling" for them as substitutes for the husband and children I do not have.

Appreciating siblinghood means mining the full depths of this relationship instead of jettisoning it upon marriage, a fear a young woman once confessed to me. Siblinghood isn't the leftovers if we don't manage to get married. In a practical and eternal sense, siblinghood is one of the relationships we have with other people that endures. Being children of common parents is the one thing that spans premortal, mortal, and postmortal experiences. It is the only relationship with other people that has this claim. If I spend my time pining for a Latter-day Saint husband (who is statistically unlikely to appear), I squander all the love, growth, and possibility waiting for me among my sibling relationships. What an inestimable loss if I did so, if I spurned the gift that is siblinghood just because it was not couplehood.

Similarly, appreciating aunthood means being grateful for my *nieces and nephews*, for the chance to love them, interact with them, and learn from them as nieces and nephews; they do not take

> **I have seen single, childless women and widowed empty nesters absorb and internalize the rhetoric that reduces all of our bountiful family experiences into one phase of family life and a phase not everyone experiences.**

the place of children I won't have. Nor could any potential children of mine take their place in my heart and my life. Being their aunt is its own emotionally, socially, and spiritually satisfying fact, one I appreciate more when I let it be what it is instead of squishing it into some lesser version of being a mother.

There is untapped power in sister-ing and aunt-ing that is lost to me, my family, my church, and my society when I or others describe family solely in terms of marriage or parenthood. And it isn't just sister-ing and aunt-ing that has unmined depths; there are deep wells of possibilities in uncle-ing, brother-ing, cousin-ing, and in-law-ing that languish or even deteriorate when we diminish or rhetorically ignore such relationships and the labors they entail. There is great potential in making claims to our other family relations. We can reclaim these rich family connections not just for recognition, but as a way of broadening our reach, as a way of drawing others to us, no matter their marital or parental status.

I have seen single, childless women and widowed empty nesters absorb and internalize the rhetoric that reduces all of our bountiful family experiences into one phase of family life and a phase not everyone experiences. They have described single life as a wasteland or wilderness, as a trial or punishment, and as a curse. Lessons are taught and talks given about family life. Rarely does the discussion call upon their own extended family experiences, but instead focuses on raising small children or getting along with a spouse. These relationships are not part

of everyone's daily life, and in many cases they are not part of others' life experience at all.[2] It is particularly striking when I've spoken to such women outside of formal church settings and discovered just how meaningful and varied their family relationships are, how much effort they put into being a sister or an aunt, experiences I have rarely, if ever, heard them share over the pulpit or in class. Additionally, expanding our view of family to include the ways it changes over a lifetime could make us more aware of what it is like to have adult children.

Appreciating a family that does not contain a spouse or children is not a compensatory act; it is an essential act, one that has to be directly advocated for. I work diligently to speak up about my family at church, to lay claim to its importance on its own terms, instead of allowing it to remain invisible or contorting it beyond recognition. Since that phone conversation over a dozen years ago, my family has experienced both joyous growth and devastating loss. We've wrestled with expectations around family reunions, faith, and concerns over health scares. We have amused ourselves nicknaming the different generations and spend time talking about the privileges and responsibilities of each generation to the other generations. We are keenly aware that perpetuating the bonds that connect and support us takes attention and intention.

In my bones and in my blood, in my joy and my heartache, I am daily grateful for the family I have. All of these people are central to me, not auxiliary, not placeholders for some unrealized, idealized future family. They are the real thing, here and now. And forever. ✳

1.   Psalm 23:5; Luke 6:38; Malachi 3:10; Doctrine and Covenants 121:45; 128:19; Romans 5:5; 1 Nephi 11:22.

2.   It was recently reported at general conference that the majority of Church members are currently single. Whether that is because someone is yet to marry, divorced, never married, or widowed, it is safe to say being single at church is a universal experience—even if it is an intermittent or short period for some people. Gerrit W. Gong, "Room in the Inn," *Liahona*, May 2021, 24–27; M. Russell Ballard, "Hope in Christ," *Liahona*, May 2021, 53–56.

SCROLLING INSTAGRAM, NOVEMBER 2023

BRINN
ELIZABETH
BAGLEY

What I used to think would tone my arms / next slide / a man crumpled on dirty concrete, someone nearby is lifting a flashlight to the dark, someone else using his arms to cut the bloodied limb – you can feel the chill, see piles of used and soiled blankets, no one is coming / everything 50 percent off! Don't miss our biggest sale of the / whole family, gone / my best secret for / being a coward, complicit and covered in safety, how dare / You guys! This set is SO comfy, grab the link / look at this mushroom I found, can you believe / I'm here again. *We are still here.* Have not slept in our beds for over a month. Our homes are rubble. *See us.* There is no food. Where are / you will never believe how I finally lost the last / 15,000 pounds of concrete, falling, the sound takes longer to reach our ears / is there any love here for my new book / poem / body / thought / loaf / outfit / my family is missing / all of this happening / five-year-olds wrapped in white bags, their mothers / 5 fun holiday recipes you have to / try carrying your dying child out into a morning with nowhere safe to go, breathing in a world that would do this.

Jorge Cocco

IS 500 PAGES TOO MUCH?

GRANT HARDY

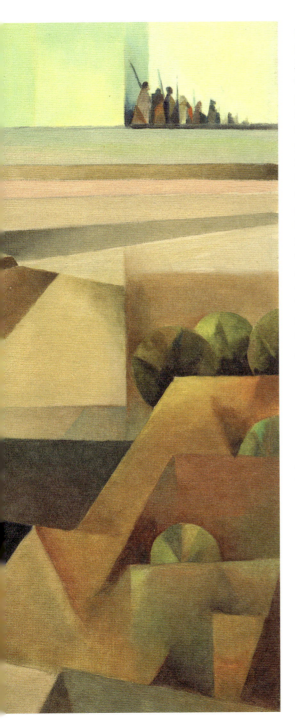

WHEN THE BOOK OF MORMON WAS first published in 1830, just eleven days before Joseph Smith formally organized the Church of Christ, it was a substantial volume—some 582 pages of dense paragraphs broken only by a few chapter and book divisions. The profusion of unfamiliar names and plotlines from a thousand years of Nephite history, ostensibly abridged from multiple plates and records, would have made it a difficult read. Nevertheless, its main message came through clearly enough, telling the story of a branch of Israel in the Americas that worshiped Christ before his birth, was visited by him after his resurrection, and then was eventually destroyed when they fell into disbelief and sin. Today the official edition has been streamlined to 530 pages, thanks to a smaller font size and double columns, but the Book of Mormon is still a challenge to read cover to cover, perhaps even more so than two hundred years ago because its archaic King James Bible–like language is increasingly foreign to contemporary English speakers.

Longtime Church members know the book's major stories from lessons, talks, and artwork, and many will have spent time with the text itself in personal or family scripture study. Latter-day Saints revere the book as "Another Testament of Jesus Christ" (a subtitle that was added in 1982), yet we tend to read it devotionally rather than analytically. That is to say, we skim its pages—not always rapidly—seeking confirmation of Moroni's promise that God will "manifest the truth of it unto you, by the power of the Holy Ghost" (Moroni 10:4), and we treat the book as evidence for Joseph Smith's prophetic calling and the authority of the church he founded. We read for familiar doctrines such as faith and repentance that we can apply to our lives, and we take comfort in its witness of Christ's atonement and his offer of resurrection and salvation. This approach is perhaps best exemplified in the *Come, Follow Me* curriculum, where the manual highlights just a few verses each week, with brief comments by General Authorities followed by invitations for reflection and discussion.

This is all good, but some readers may wonder why it takes five hundred pages to convey these points. How would our experience with the Book of Mormon be different if all we had was, say, 1 Nephi 1–18 and 3 Nephi 11–27 stitched together with a few comments from Mormon, and then

> If a few chapters and selected quotations from the Book of Mormon are all that it takes to gain a testimony and learn the basic doctrines of the Restoration, why is the Book of Mormon so long and convoluted, when it might have been as short as the Bhagavad Gita, or a compilation of wisdom sayings like the Dhammapada or the Daodejing?

Moroni 4–5, and 10 tacked onto the end—a bit less than one hundred pages? We might miss several beloved tales (which could be replaced by incidents from the Bible or Church history), but we would still have inspiring stories, the basic principles of the gospel, the sacrament prayers, and prophecies of the latter days. A drastically reduced Book of Mormon would still testify of Christ, and translating a one-hundred-page text from gold plates by means of the Urim and Thummim would be just as miraculous as translating five hundred pages. In short, there seems to be a mismatch between what the Book of Mormon is and how we use it.

This is not simply a thought experiment. Currently, high school students need only read

twenty-two chapters to receive seminary credit for an entire year (1 Nephi 1; 8; 11; 2 Nephi 9:1–29; Mosiah 2–5; Alma 5; 7; 32–34; 3 Nephi 11; 15–21; Moroni 10). Similarly, the institute manual *Teachings and Doctrine of the Book of Mormon* asks college students to look at about forty scattered verses, roughly the equivalent of a chapter and a half, for each of its twenty-eight lessons. If, as these courses suggest, a few chapters and selected quotations from the Book of Mormon are all that it takes to gain a testimony and learn the basic doctrines of the Restoration, why is the Book of Mormon so long and convoluted, when it might have been as short as the Bhagavad Gita, or a compilation of wisdom sayings like the Dhammapada or the Daodejing? Indeed, it might have been more appealing to outsiders, and certainly easier for young people to grasp.

In general, we tend to read the Book of Mormon instrumentally, as a means to receive personal revelation, to form a commitment to Joseph Smith and The Church of Jesus Christ of Latter-day Saints, and to affirm our understanding of basic Christian concepts and the teachings of Church leaders. These are important functions, yet the Book of Mormon was designed for a different type of reading—one that recognizes and responds to its well-crafted, intricate narrative. (In this respect, the Nephite record is quite different from the compilation of short, independent revelations that is the Doctrine and Covenants, or the revised biblical chapters in the Pearl of Great Price.) What would it look like to read the Book of Mormon as a gift from God, in which every word and phrase was potentially significant, where its basic structure was seen as an integral part of its message? How might things be different if our approach to this sacred text focused more on divine priorities rather than our personal needs and desires?

To take just one example, we might examine 2 Nephi 25–30. These chapters play an important role in the overall design of Nephi's book. After reproducing a sermon by his younger brother Jacob on Isaiah 49–51 (2 Nephi 6–10), Nephi inserted an eight-verse introduction before quoting Isaiah 2–14 in full (2 Nephi 11–24), replicating the King James Version with a few

Jorge Cocco

intriguing variants. The prophecies of Isaiah obviously mattered a great deal to Nephi, who is depicted as poring over them meticulously, looking for God's will concerning his chosen people and all of humankind. (By contrast, how often do Latter-day Saints quickly skim over these chapters, ignoring their historical and literary significance, sometimes not even recognizing that they were originally written as poetry?) In chapters 25–30, Nephi interweaves his own prophecies with those of Jacob and Isaiah, thus confirming the truth of his words through multiple witnesses (see 2 Nephi 11:2–4). These textual interconnections can be traced through phrasal repetitions and allusions. Here are just a few examples:

26:1 Nephi refers to "my beloved brethren" for the first time, adopting an expression that Jacob used thirteen times in chapters 6–10; Nephi will employ this phrase fifteen more times through the end of 2 Nephi.

26:7 Nephi exclaims, "Thy ways are just," thus reconciling himself to the will of God (as advised by Jacob at 10:24) regarding the future destruction of his posterity, despite the pain and anguish he had borne since his vision many years earlier (see 1 Nephi 15:5).

26:14–19 Nephi interprets Isaiah 29:3–5 (originally referring to a siege of Jerusalem in 701 BC) by recontextualizing its words within a prophecy concerning the Lamanites and the coming forth of the Book of Mormon in the last days. Somewhat remarkably, this is done through insertions into a phrase-by-phrase recitation of the original Isaiah passage.

Jorge Cocco

27:26 Nephi adds the words *and learned* to Isaiah 29:14 ("for the wisdom of their wise and learned shall perish"), thus connecting Isaiah's prophecy with Jacob's words at 2 Nephi 9:28 ("when they are learned they think they are wise").

29:1 The Lord picks up Nephi's combining of Isaiah 11:11 and 29:14 at 2 Nephi 25:14 (in reverse order), before continuing with additional quotations from Isaiah—something more easily seen than described.

> NEPHI: *And the Lord will set his hand again the second time to restore his people* from their lost and fallen state. Wherefore, he will proceed *to do a marvelous work and a wonder* among the children of men. (2 Nephi 25:14, with Isaiah phrases in italics)

> THE LORD: But behold there shall be many—at *that day when I shall proceed to do a marvelous work among them,* that I may remember my covenants which I have made unto the children of men, that I may *set my hand again the second time to recover my people* which are of the house of Israel. (2 Nephi 29:1)

In addition, the regular interactions with the King James Bible seen in 2 Nephi 25–30 make these chapters something of a biblical commentary. When Nephi alludes to the story of the brass serpent at 25:20, observing that the Lord "gave unto Moses power that he should heal the nations," he makes the miracle of Numbers 21:4–9 applicable to all humankind, not just Israel. At 25:24–30, Nephi's understanding of the law of Moses is similar to Paul's, regarding it as a set of temporary commandments having their fulfillment and termination in Christ (see Romans 7:1–6; 10:4; Galatians 3:24–26), yet where Paul proclaims that Christians are dead to the law (Romans 7:4; Galatians 2:19), Nephi asserts that the law itself will be dead for believers. And Nephi transforms God's general summons at Isaiah 55:1 into a personal invitation to come to Christ at 2 Nephi 26:25 ("Come unto me all ye ends of the earth"), in the process replacing Isaiah's "wine and milk" with *milk and honey,* a common biblical description of the bounties of the promised land.

Throughout 2 Nephi 25–30, it becomes clear that Nephi, though he has been granted extraordinary revelations and visions, is nevertheless a very careful reader of scripture, and he is also capable of listening to and learning from his younger brother—unlike Laman and Lemuel. He realizes that many of the prophecies in Isaiah 12–24, especially those concerning political events, had already been fulfilled by his own day, while others were still pending. One of his arguments is that the reliability of Isaiah's predictions for the eighth century BC should lend credence to prophecies still to be realized (see 2 Nephi 25:6–8). Readers are invited to view Nephi's writings in light of his struggles and frustrations with his family, his concerns for his descendants and future readers, his silence regarding his many years as king, and his developing understanding of God's plan for humanity. Why else would Nephi's words have been provided such a thick narrative context?

This mode of reading—identifying major textual components and how they fit together, looking for repetition and allusions, connecting everything to the broader narrative in the context of the writer's life and intentions, with painstaking attention to individual words and phrases—is not what we are taught in Sunday School, seminary, or institute, much less in popular podcasts and blog posts. Yet approaching the Book of Mormon in this way, constantly asking questions, can take us deeper into the narrative, revealing a richness and nuance to the remarkable scripture that God had given us in this particular form. There is much more to Nephi than many readers of 1 Nephi first assume. Similarly, as we learn more about other Nephite prophets and writers, and about Christ himself through both his words and his guidance to the narrators, we can begin to appreciate the Book of Mormon as a gift. We may even begin to feel gratitude to have over five hundred pages of the kind of scripture that repays this type of close attention.

Fortunately for Latter-day Saints, there are precedents that we can draw upon. For several centuries Jews and Christians have read the

Bible in astonishing detail, often with admirable religious insight, and frequently aided by historical-critical and textual studies. (The Hebrew Bible, especially, both respects and expects critical thinking from its readers.) The Book of Mormon and the Bible are not identical in how they function as history and literature, but there is enough overlap that several of the most useful and insightful approaches in biblical scholarship can be applied to the Mormon scripture. A good place to begin is with academic study Bibles such as those published by HarperCollins, including the recently released SBL *Study Bible* (from the Society of Biblical Literature), and by Oxford University Press, which has produced the *New Oxford Annotated Bible,* the *Jewish Study Bible,* and the *Catholic Study Bible.* In that same tradition, I edited the *Annotated Book of Mormon,* published by Oxford earlier this year, from which all the examples above are taken. This is the first nonbiblical scripture ever published by OUP's Bible Division (as befits a sacred text, all my editor's royalties will be donated to the Church's Humanitarian Aid Fund).

There are, to be sure, anachronisms and implausibilities in the Book of Mormon, and even passages where the Nephites and their prophets do not always live up to their ideals, yielding instead to what we might regard today as materialism, militarism, racism, and sexism. (There are lessons both positive and negative within its pages.) Yet the close study of this revealed text, in the entirety of its length and form, can bring us closer to God. Nephi, Jacob, Alma, Mormon, and Moroni are some of the wisest, most thoughtful, most spiritually mature voices in our religious tradition. By coming to know them through a detailed study of their struggles and encounters with divinity, as conveyed in their writings and editing, we can come to know Christ. The Book of Mormon is much more than is strictly necessary for a basic understanding of Christian principles and a testimony of Joseph Smith. It is one of the most miraculous elements of the Restoration, a self-revelation of God that apparently could not be adequately conveyed in less than five hundred pages. ✳

CONSIDER THE—

ROBBIE
TAGGART

i.

ravens—the way their dark eyes reflect
your own death, how when you look up
through a hole in their wings you become
one of them—specters, the souls of wicked
priests, thought and memory blueblack
in body

Consider also their raucous teenage years,
the anxious excrement of loneliness
hoping for the one right bird to fly
alongside forever

Or ponder the baffling things they do—
the ways they smash up ants in their beaks
and smear them all over their lustrous
plumage like some healing balm

Consider how dim is our knowledge
of small things like birds

ii.

I bet you thought I was going to say "lilies"
basking in God's given goodness, naked
as the day you were born, unashamed,
unencumbered no-spin-straight,
lazy as avocado toast slow morning
confident as Solomon
in shimmering new robes

But Jesus was always slanting
expectations, spinning koans
out of earthy air

I have come to launch a fire
into the midst of existence
What's my purpose if everything
is already burning?

iii.

I was thinking myself a cubit taller,
imagining each inch's upward stretch
when I looked up to see an unkindness
of ravens plowing their fields, whistling
their contentment with the day, mimicking
the soft laughter of farmhands at labor

They pushed each seed snugly into the
black dirt with passerine deftness
and flocked to help a fellow
raise a barn

Weary with the work of ingathering
they hunkered home to conspire
around a table so sturdy
it must have been built
by God

iv.

The bakers and bringers
of Elijah's bread, perfecters
of the art of sourdough, are telling
jokes and everyone's laughing

v.

Consider what you love
and how you spend
your finite hours
through the stark
eyes of those who
trust
      life
                           like
                    these
dark
            birds

(Inspired by Luke 12:24–27, 49)

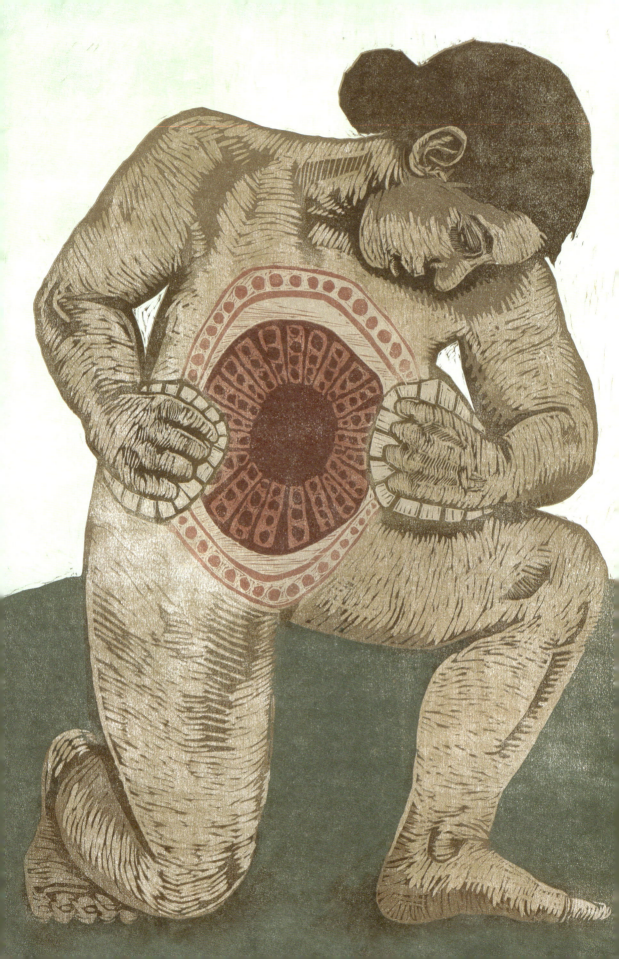

AN EXPANSE OF LIGHT & MEMORY

On Mothering & Being Mothered

CHARLOTTE WILSON

I CAN'T REMEMBER THE FIRST year of my daughter's life. I think, write, say those words and my chest tightens, grief and shame washing through my body. I can't remember.

I can't remember.

The hazy recesses of memory recall an urgent call to Heavenly Mother around this time. Maybe my spirit subconsciously knew to prepare for impending darkness, or perhaps I felt heightened stakes of raising a daughter in a world still burdened with patriarchy, but finding my Mother felt a life-and-death effort. If I didn't find Her, would I ever find myself?

Eve came first, though, the Ursa Major guiding me to Polaris. Eve and her choices both fascinated and perplexed me. For years I'd wondered why God would give a commandment to Eve and Adam that they were destined to break, and why, if the Fall was both inevitable and essential, we would talk about Eve being tempted and deceived, when to me she clearly had the foresight and courage to be the first to step over the threshold into the unknown. With time, the temple endowment confirmed what I intuitively knew about Eve, but still I wondered: if we were to properly revere her, what changes would we see in how women interacted in and with our world? And furthermore, what parts of myself were already in a metamorphosis for simply choosing this knowledge?

Seeking Eve opened my heart to the divine feminine and unlocked spiritual access that had never been taught or explained to me. Connecting with Eve filled me with conviction, vision, and purpose. She taught me to take ownership of my spirituality and that my access to my Heavenly Parents is mine alone to claim.

I didn't know how sick I was until about a year postpartum. Darkness had steadily filled my periphery, manifesting as panic attacks, bursts of rage, and deepening wells of shame. I would see my friends parent their broods of children with seeming ease and wonder what I was doing wrong—maybe I really was this bad at mothering more than one. My narrow preconceptions

To say that I found Heavenly Mother wouldn't be entirely correct. She found me, touching my raw and desperate soul just enough to remind me that She was there.

about postpartum mental health kept my insights limited and my options few. My husband, a daily witness to this gradual and dark descent, didn't know what signs to watch for or even what questions to ask. We both were lost in the dark, not even knowing the lights had gone out.

I didn't know what to make of my pounding heart and consistently tight chest, my inability to breathe fully or slowly, the daily dread I felt upon waking. Outwardly I faked a brave and tired smile, assuring myself and others that things were fine, because what else was I supposed to say? Sometimes I believed myself.

The labor turned dire in what felt like an instant. I had an epidural and was hoping to steal a couple hours' rest in the midnight hospital room before my daughter would stake her claim in the world. We breathed easier when we turned off the overhead fluorescents, calming ourselves in the simple glow from the sconce wall lighting. The nurse came in just as I was about to fall into a medicated doze.

"Could we move you to your side maybe?" she asked. She wedged an inflatable bean-shaped pillow between my legs, and I realized with resignation that I wouldn't be sleeping any more that night. I glanced at the heart rate printing out on the machine next to the bed.

"What's wrong?" I asked. "Do I need to be worried?"

"Oh, nothing we haven't seen before!" the nurse replied, a little too upbeat to be convincing. A tense, unspoken current of doubt cut through the conversation. I glanced at my husband for reassurance just as his eyes darted to mine, needing the same.

My baby's heartbeat was irregular, changing with each contraction. The nurse moved my numb legs around, trying to position my body and uterus such that my daughter's heart rate would stabilize, hoping that steadying her pulse would be an easy fix.

Time in labor contracts and dilates, and I don't remember the doctor coming in. In one memory, the room is dim and sleepy, and the next is buzzing with fluorescent light, beeping machines, and a cadre of nurses in constant motion. That cozy glow of pre-baby anticipation shattered as the hospital reminded me that this was no place for comfort. I was here to do a job, and my daughter's life depended on it.

I couldn't feel anything, not my legs, not even that singular urge to bear down and push. But I pushed when they told me to. Her heart rate continued to fluctuate. The nurses, once personable and encouraging, flipped to professional and clinical as if on a switch. I was a body in a bed, divorced from my mind and heart.

"You have one more chance to push this baby out," they told me. One more chance before emergency measures would activate.

I pushed one last time and entered a liminal space, neither here nor there. The hospital room faded around me, and I felt, rather than saw, a tunnel full of light, a glowing nebula of potential and power. The light here was soft and kind and full, quiet and pulsing with purpose. Mothers lined the tunnel, the veil parting as they held fast to each other, channeling their combined power and all-consuming love directly into me. My grandmothers, their mothers, the Mother of all Living, my Mother—we were all together in that place that isn't a space, connected in mind, body, and soul, infusing love and life into every breath and cry.

She came. My daughter came, and her heart beat the way it should. But my womb still bled.

Sarah Winegar

Blood with no source spilled onto the tiled floor, my vision blurred, yet I felt still connected to that tunnel built with love and sustained with strength. My daughter had arrived, but I had yet to follow. The matriarchs still held me, maintaining the celestial connections woven between us and my earthside infant, the stardust in the air preserving, protecting, and saving.

I don't know what happened to stanch the bleeding, what anyone did to save my body. Whatever it was left my limbs shaking, the connection between my mind and body crooked and wounded. And that beautiful tunnel had closed, closing off part of my mind and heart with it.

We went home and entered the timeless newborn vortex of midnights and feedings and swollen belly and breasts, tears that can't be named as happy or sad or even tired. Life went on and yet was entirely changed. And I didn't know who I was or how to be anymore. I cared for both my daughter and my toddler son, trying to hold on to the breaking pieces of myself.

I can't tell you much about that year, because those months gave no room for those moments to root into memory. They are seeds thrown on thorny, stony ground. I have photos and even video to prove that these moments happened. But were I to try and recall my own life with my baby, I could not, my memories a fallen rung on a ladder.

To say that I found Heavenly Mother wouldn't be entirely correct. She found me, touching my raw and desperate soul just enough to remind me that She was there, that the tunnel of light that had once enveloped me hadn't completely closed. She met me in the fourth watch, holding us both tight to her breast as I rocked my baby girl in the pre-dawn. She held me when my sick mind cut off my energy and feeling. She moved in the background, asking for nothing but to love me. I don't remember the moment when I entered the eye of the storm and could clearly see the raging winds surrounding me. But I do recall knowing what to do. What to say and to ask, who to tell.

The mothers caught them, stood under the falling stars and held fast to every drop and beam of light that I had lost.

When I finally gasped that desperate cry for help, my Mother was the first to grasp my flailing hand, keeping me from drifting even further into the depth of the tempest, promising me deliverance.

Slowly, surely I recovered. Maybe even healed a little.

I write this as my almost eight-year-old daughter laughs downstairs, leaping into an intrepid game of make-believe with her brothers, abandoning her intricate art project for later. Her joie de vivre fills our home like sunshine pouring through a southern window. I try to hold on to every moment of her kindness and curiosity and solar energy, marveling at the gift of our converging orbits. Our Mother's love shimmers on all the gossamer strands connecting my daughter and me, making our mutual affection glimmer and shine so that, when I'm with her, heaven is always in the periphery.

But those first twelve months are still dark matter, unknowable and unreachable.

I don't remember—
and yet.

At some point beyond my grasp of memory, a chain of strength and love reignited through my bones and tissues a cellular memory of that in-between space I once visited, the space filled with light and mothers. And just as I know that every day we turn back toward the sun, I knew that all the memories I thought I'd lost were not lost at all. My host of progenitors, all of us linked through our very cells—daughter to daughter to daughter, folding over and back again to Mother, crossing continents, planets, light-years through infinite, nameless suns—these women of wisdom and love now safeguard my daughter's tender infancy, those moments my mind had to release in a last-ditch effort to survive.

The mothers caught them, stood under the falling stars and held fast to every drop and beam of light that I had lost.

She will restore those memories to me. Someday. She pulls them out, relives them, keeping them alive and breathing for me, loving them the way a mother counts every finger and toe on her newborn babe, promising a restoration more intimate and tender than I'd ever dared to dream. We speak of restoration, and yet do we really think we can understand the depth and breadth of the restoration our Mother intends? Perhaps the miracle of the Restoration isn't constrained to an institution or scripture, but rather the knowledge of singular wholeness beyond healing, a personal deliverance curated to a single, broken soul. Restoration, not just of the world, but of me, as a daughter. Countless single, broken souls spangled across the heavens, all of us shooting out light hoping to be seen, all delivered by a Son beloved by His Mother.

She holds all my broken pieces, old scars and fresh wounds, eagerly waiting for my day of restoration, when I, with my daughter and her daughters, can walk through that tunnel of light into a star, into the arms of all the mothers who ever loved us, an expanse irradiating hope and wholeness enough to expand our ever-expanding universe, a restoration reassuring me I have always been known. ✳

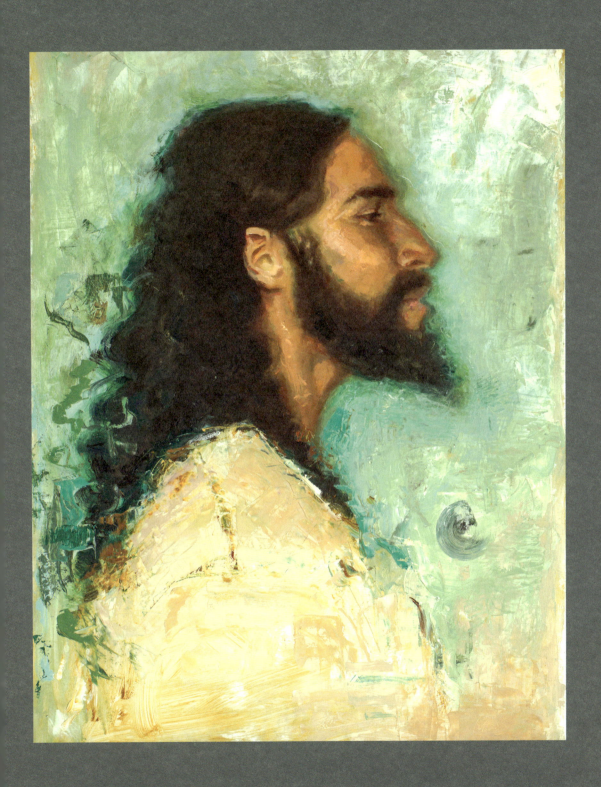

Living Waters

JENNA HURST CONLIN

BENEATH THE TREE

STEPHEN CARTER

Artwork by Mark England

Some people have never seen stars.

I certainly hadn't.

I had always lived beneath the tree, the fruit swaying above my head. To look up was to bathe in their light. To pick one was to grasp a bright jewel. To bite into it was to drink molten.

Everything outside that golden space was hidden tides. Unknown paths. Ravenous earth. Anyone who wandered there was lost. But beneath the tree we were safe. Nourished.

At one end of that little land was the rod of iron, emerging from the dark and then, reaching the tree's perimeter, suddenly turning upward, stretching into the sky. Someone was always watching over the rod in case a figure coalesced from the mist—running to meet them and supporting their final steps toward the tree. All to watch the look that came over their face, the golden glow that spread through their body, as they took their first bite.

But at the other end of our circle was the building, jutting crookedly from the ground, leaning over us. People called to us from its openings. Some of our brave ones went near to engage with them—answering their arguments, returning their mockery.

I never went too near. I never ventured outside the arms of the tree. It was home.

But one day.

(How do I put this?)

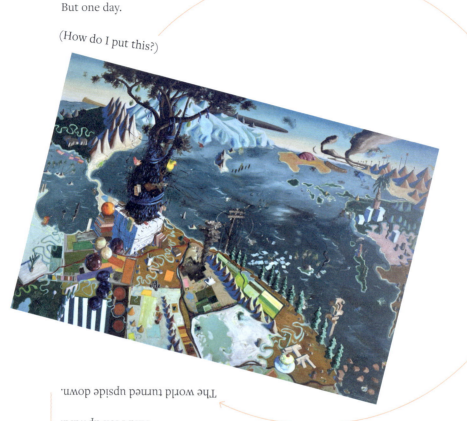

The world turned upside down.

And I fell upward.

I grabbed at the branches as I fell, trying desperately to save myself. But every branch I caught either slid out of my grasp or broke. Finally, I burst through the top of the tree, and saw darkness.

My home sunk away beneath me as I flailed in the empty air.

Then the gray angle of the building slid into view. I realized that it was close enough to grab. I could save myself! I could climb into the building, find my way to the bottom, and back to the tree. And, indeed, I caught hold of an opening and clung to it.

I looked up at the abyss I had just saved myself from and stared.

Sprinkled in the blackness were—

I remembered a person I had seen lying beneath the tree, arms crossed behind head, staring upward. The person intrigued me because they seemed to have a different glow than the golden one that suffused the others.

"What are you looking at?" I asked.

"Stars," they replied.

I had never heard that word before, and they seemed to know it.

"Imagine," they said, "that you took the seeds from a thousand shining fruits and threw them upward. And they stayed in the sky, glowing."

They looked at me. "Seeds have life."

And as I clung to the building, I saw the seeds in the sky. They were beautiful.

But so far away.

I looked at the building, at my tree, and then at the stars.

And I let go.

It was terrifying. I had no ground. No gravity. No direction. And my tree diminished beneath me until it was simply one star among millions.

I don't know how long I fell. But eventually, I saw something familiar. A rod of iron stretching across my path. I grabbed and held onto it desperately, certain that it would bring me back to my tree. But which way would I have to go to find it? I finally chose a direction and pulled myself through emptiness, grateful for this one strand of reality to follow.

Soon I was pulling myself through mists, and then waters, and then marsh— the land slowly solidifying beneath me. And I saw a glow ahead. A tree with shining fruit. I wept as I struggled toward it. Soon, an arm wrapped itself around my shoulders and helped me along the final steps to the tree. I reached up and plucked the fruit, taking an ardent bite and swallowing.

I almost choked. I looked at the fruit in my hand. It was different. Had a different glow. Taste. Texture. I wanted to throw it away from me. To dash back out into the darkness. To find the real thing. But as the fruit spread through my body, I felt it nourishing me. And I knew that it was good. My glow started to shift.

I stayed a long time beneath that new tree. Reveling in its fruit. Hungry for its taste. Disdainful of the people in the building who mocked me. All thought of my previous tree sank to the back of my mind. This was the right place.

And then. The world turned upside down. I was wrested from this tree the way I was wrested from the first. And again, I was lost among stars. Grief-stricken. A part of me started turning as dark as the space around me. I raged into the emptiness.

But then, another rod of iron. And, of course, I took it. I wanted somewhere to stand. Anywhere.

And I found. Another tree. Another fruit. Another joy.

Look at the stars up there. All those seeds. All those trees.

I search the sky. Find that one particular golden star.

And feel a tug.

Why? I have the whole universe.

I look at my hand. My original glow has been suffused with many other colors. Would anyone at home even recognize me?

Would I even want to be around them? It's such a small place.

I remember all the people who had emerged from the mists holding on to the rod of iron. Who were they? I had assumed that they had simply been born in those mists. But now I knew that they could have come from anywhere. Tasted anything.

Who were the people I had lived among for so long? Had any of them fallen upward as I had?

Of course.

One had told me about stars.

And even those who had never been torn from the tree. What deep knowledge pooled in them that I, a traveler, cannot gather?

What about those in the building? Had they inadvertently aborted their fall, clinging to the stability of the building, just as I had wanted to?

What about those like me, who need to know—

"What are you looking at?" someone asks. ✳

STUMBLING OVER SEER STONES

The Redeeming Strangeness of the Book of Mormon

JAMES EGAN

SCANDALOUS ORIGINS

A FEW YEARS AGO, DURING MY first visit to the revamped Church History Museum, I happened to overhear a conversation between two recently returned missionaries as they read about the role of seer stones in the translation of the Book of Mormon, apparently for the first time.[1] As they took in the exhibit's large picture of Joseph Smith's swirly, chocolate-colored stone, one turned to the other and asked, "So how'd it work?" The answer: a nervous laugh, then a shared shrug.

Religious history is full of the odd and extraordinary, but Smith's translation of the Book of Mormon is often seen as especially strange. Some of his contemporaries thought his claims so absurd they worried the Book of Mormon was "an atheistic plot to discredit all religion."[2] Many "knowing men" saw themselves as duty bound to stop such nefarious schemes and yet assured each other that the only people who took interest were the "unlettered," believers in ghosts, goblins, and witchcraft.[3] More recently, the claims are regularly mocked as crazy, if mostly harmless, in the musical *The Book of Mormon*.

Of course, then as now, bright, educated people have believed Smith's story. But Latter-day Saints often share incredulity about his audacious claims, if only privately and with a different sort of apprehension and intensity. Is it really reasonable to believe them? And if so, how? To all of us, believers and skeptics, Joseph Smith expressed his sympathy: "I don't blame anyone for not believing my history; if I had not experienced what I have I could not have believed it myself."[4]

Despite such permission to admit perplexity, Latter-day Saints often seek to normalize or divert attention from the Book of Mormon's unsettling origins. We emphasize how participation in folk magic was fairly common in Smith's time and place.[5] We argue that his engagement in it was necessary preparation for the supernatural events of the Restoration.[6] We point to strange stories in the Bible or peculiarities in other traditions' histories.[7] And we worry that preoccupation with seer stones diverts our attention from the subtlety and power of the text.[8]

These various responses to the scandal of the Book of Mormon are understandable, and they

> **God challenges us to live with an eye toward a heavenly world that is deeply and mysteriously intertwined with our own.**

can be an effective means of encouraging readers of all kinds to take the book seriously. But what would happen if we leaned into the strangeness of seer stones and other bewildering details of the book's production? What if, in those disorienting details, we find help with the divine work the book's words call us to join? What if our embarrassment and discomfort are central to the book's purposes, a vital feature of its power to connect us to Christ, which also means to each other—the convicted and incredulous both?

To see what we might gain from embracing the strange, we have to first see the scandal in the New Testament's sense of the term. A *skandalon*, the Greek term often translated as "stumbling block," is a confusing, even offensive, surprise. Paul uses the term in an explanation to the Corinthians of Christ's crucifixion: "We preach Christ crucified, unto the Jews a *stumbling-block*, and unto the Greeks foolishness."[9] And he explains that the purpose of this challenging foolishness is to unify the human family in humility: "God chose the foolish things of the world to shame the wise; God chose the weak things of the world to shame the strong; God chose the insignificant and despised things of the world— yes, even things that don't exist—to abolish the power of the things that do exist, so that no creature could boast in God's presence."[10]

Falling over a stumbling block prepares us to be reoriented and remade, which is the aim of Joseph Smith's broader project of translation. As Samuel Brown argues, the project included the Book of Mormon, the New Translation of the Bible, large sections of the Doctrine and Covenants, the Book of Moses, the Book of Abraham, and the temple liturgy, and its aim was to transform what the Bible means—that is, what it does—to its readers.[11] For Smith, the Bible was "a precious

trace of the . . . presence of God and a . . . conduit to communion with the ancient authors," and its readers, whether they believed it to be an inerrant universal text or a flawed regional history, were cut off from the conduit.[12] The point of Smith's project was to reconnect readers to that presence of God and their ancestors and gather them into a "simultaneous human family."[13]

Adding to Brown's argument, I want to suggest that the mechanisms of translation may be an indispensable catalyst for the intended collective transformation, especially as the Book of Mormon's seer stones are concerned. In his adaptation of a practice (folk magic) valorized by the unschooled for its material promise and demonized by the literate for its "mystical" pretensions, God frees us from prisons of class division and worldly wisdom as much as those of time and space. And by calling Smith to dig up gold plates only to return them to heaven, God challenges us to live with an eye toward a heavenly world that is deeply and mysteriously intertwined with our own.

THE FUNCTION OF THE SKANDALON: RECONCILING THE WISE AND THE FOOLISH

If we look away from the Book of Mormon's bewildering birth too quickly, we may look past the way the unsophisticated (the Joseph Smiths of the world) are deeply connected to the well-being of the wise, and how God is calling us to be "familiar with all."[14] We may fail to fully appreciate the way God is at work in the weakness among us and how he calls us out of small mindedness, using simple means to bring about remarkable things.[15] Various passages in the book itself challenge us to consider how we are prone to resist these calls and how its peculiar origins will make them difficult for many to hear. The book seems profoundly aware that those who feel convicted by its claims will be put into a new, controversial relationship with the world, perhaps especially if they are, as the text would put it, "learned."

The clearest example of this self-consciousness is Nephi's application of Isaiah 29 to the origins of the Book of Mormon. He uses Isaiah's talk of sealed prophecy to describe the Book of Mormon, whose power is essentially sealed off from the learned because they will not read it, leaving the power to be experienced by the unlearned. Latter-day Saints commonly read this passage as an anticipation of Martin Harris's encounter with Charles Anthon, but as Joseph Spencer argues, Nephi has a larger group in mind.[16] Spencer emphasizes the plural pronoun Nephi uses in expressing God's response to the refusal of the learned to read the book: "Then shall the Lord God say unto him: The learned shall not read them, for *they* have rejected them, and I am able to do mine own work; wherefore thou shalt read the words which I shall give unto thee."[17]

It is tempting for contemporary believers to read this "they" as a reference to secular atheists, but the people Nephi appears to have in mind are the educated and pious who think they understand God's ways. The next verses quote Isaiah 29:13–14: "Forasmuch as this people draw near unto me with their mouth, and with their lips do honor me, but have removed their hearts far from me, and their fear towards me is taught by the precepts of men—Therefore, I will proceed to do a marvelous work among this people, yea, a marvelous work and a wonder, for the wisdom of their wise and learned shall perish, and the understanding of their prudent shall be hid."[18] These people try to escape or control God's marvelous work by overconfident interpretation of scripture, so God produces more of it, and by unnerving means.

Nephi describes the translation of the Book of Mormon by turning Isaiah's image of a whispering ghost from the underworld (a "familiar spirit" in the King James Version) into a picture of divine, intergenerational communication.[19] On his account, the whispering is ignored by the learned, who build many churches but dismiss the power of God. Thinking themselves wise and capable enough to do the work of God without his power, they stumble "because of the greatness of their stumbling block," which is perhaps the Book of Mormon itself.[20]

God sends the Book of Mormon to them not merely to address their pride, but to combat the way it divides the human family. As Nephi sees it, the learned's attempt to control sacred text and God's work has higher stakes than arcane theological debate. The effect is to turn churches, even religion itself, into a project of self-aggrandizement resulting in factionalism and division: "Their churches have become corrupted, and their churches are lifted up; because of pride they are puffed up. They rob the poor because of their fine sanctuaries; they rob the poor because of their fine clothing; and they persecute the meek and the poor in heart, because in their pride they are puffed up."[21]

J. Kirk Richards

The Book of Mormon, Nephi sees, will enter this contentious, unequal world and "hiss forth" without much success because many are confident they know how God works in the world, or more specifically, because they want comfort and control rather than God's challenging word. The Bible, then, becomes something to possess rather than something to be possessed by: "A Bible! A Bible! We have got a Bible!" They do not reject the words of the book as much as the *event* of the book—its production, its claims to sacred history, its disruptive claim to the status of scripture. The Book of Mormon reasserts the transformative, unmanageable nature of scripture and its transformative demands. The learned resist this work and resist the interdependence it requires. They ignore, for instance, the way their Bible flows from the history of people they refuse to integrate and appreciate: "And what thank they the Jews for the Bible which they receive from them?" [22]

J. Kirk Richards

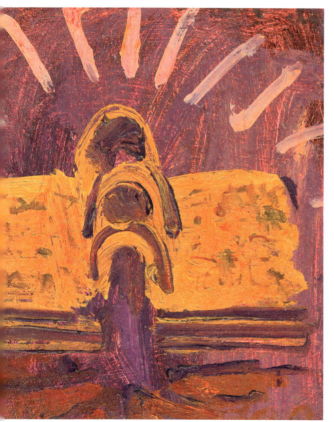

To confront these problems of pride, division, and inequality, God decides to confound the learned, or to quote my Jewish Study Bible's translation of the verses Nephi is working with, to "baffle [the] people with bafflement upon bafflement" so "the wisdom of its wise shall fail, and the prudence of its prudent shall vanish." [23] To save the learned from their self-importance that stands in the way of justice and reconciliation, he has to work with the unlearned to reveal his power and aims in startling ways—new scripture through unexpected means (seer stones) and an unsophisticated messenger (Joseph Smith).

But limited as the learned may be, God has his eyes on the weaknesses of the unlearned as well, and the details of the Book of Mormon's translation help us appreciate this too. The folk magic in which the unlearned Smith participated involved not only weird and implausible claims but also a shadowy, greedy side. His connection to "money digging" is inextricably linked to his translation of the Book of Mormon, and without a sense of the conniving secrecy of that world, we miss the way God ennobled a lowly and lost soul.

Smith's association with treasure hunting threatened production of the Book of Mormon. His First Vision set him on a new path, but his self-interested seeking after entertaining thrills and wealth kept hold of him well after he learned of the plates. As he recounts in his official history, "I was left to all kinds of temptations and, mingling with all kinds of society, I frequently fell into many foolish errors and displayed the weakness of youth, and the foibles of human nature; which, I am sorry to say, led me into divers temptations, offensive in the sight of God." [24] The society he has in mind here likely includes fellow money diggers, some of whom felt their shared enterprise entitled them to the gold plates, enough that they tried to violently steal the plates from him. Lust for riches among some of Smith's associates was, evidently, quite strong. [25]

The angel Moroni understood Smith's connection to this society and saw his need to leave its small, shallow world behind. During that first night of visitations, he warned Smith that the plates could not be obtained by one seeking riches. Yet, as Oliver Cowdery recounts (in a history Smith read and approved), by the time Smith arrived at the Hill Cumorah, "the certainty of wealth and ease in this life, had so powerfully wrought upon him" that Moroni's warning "had entirely gone from his recollection." Smith tried to take possession of the plates but was prevented as "a shock was produced upon his system, by an invisible power which deprived him in a measure, of his natural strength."[26] This would not be the last time he would be prevented from obtaining them. Joseph returned on the same date, year after year, finally securing them on his fifth try.[27]

Brigham Young is reported to have described the process of acquiring the plates as one in which God deliberately used Smith's interest in riches to lead him to higher pursuits. In Young's telling, God initially told Smith only that there was "treasure in the earth" that he wanted him to possess, and later led him along "day after day week after week year after year" until he produced the Book of Mormon. Only gradually did Smith realize that the Book of Mormon was the promised treasure.[28]

Despite Smith's significant transformation, some features of folk-magic culture survived. He remained, for example, interested in relics of the dead and spoke approvingly of seer stones up until his death.[29] But through the production of the Book of Mormon, he turned decisively away from what might have been a life of avarice and frivolity, of desire for ease and a thrill-seeking spirituality. And in this turning, God revealed to both Smith's contemporaries and to us today the emptiness of his prior aims.

What's more, God revealed what he can do with flawed material and how human desires can be elevated and refined. Through producing the Book of Mormon, Smith developed a profound commitment to the life of the mind. Rather than merely boasting of his translation powers and thumbing his nose at the learned, Smith worked to join them. Though he had given modern readers an ancient book without aid of schooling or scholarship, he sat down to study Hebrew and Egyptian. His methods were not always conventional, but he sought teachers, pursuing learning rather than dismissing it.[30] In seeking treasure, he looked for excitement and material security, but in seeking God, he found a noble quest for intelligence and communion with the human family across time, space, and class.

STRANGENESS FOR THE SAKE OF ZION

God's use of early American folk culture in bringing about the Book of Mormon, then, might be an essential feature of, rather than a distraction from, his marvelous work and wonder. By choosing Smith, he revealed not only the limits of the learned but also his power to pull the unlearned out of their foolishness. The foolish who partner with him learn the glory of intelligence just as the learned become as children, astonished out of their smugness and self-satisfaction.[31] More importantly, he revealed that the learned and unlearned need one another. Perhaps the point of calling Smith in his weirdness is not merely to

> God revealed what he can do with flawed material and how human desires can be elevated and refined.

convince us that mystical things like seer stones exist, as if that in itself were a significant step in heaven's direction. Rather, the purpose is to loosen the hold of misguided and often unconscious convictions that impede the building of redeeming relationships.

If the Book of Mormon is true, the wise need the foolish and the unlearned need the learned. If it is trustworthy, God is at work in the cosmos, which contains realities incomprehensible to every human being. If it is real, we should not be surprised that even believers wonder. As Smith's wife Emma explained years after his death and in the face of compelling personal reasons to doubt him, witnessing the book's miraculous reality didn't make it any more believable. "Joseph Smith," she told one of their sons, "could neither write nor dictate a coherent and well-worded letter, let alone . . . a book like the Book of Mormon. And, though I was an active participant in the scenes that transpired, and was present during the translation of the plates, . . . it is marvelous to me, 'a marvel and a wonder' as much so as to any one else."[32] A challenging awe, not comfortable certainty, is what we should expect from experience with the divine power that brought about the Book of Mormon.

"By the power of God," Smith proclaimed just before his death, "I translated the Book of Mormon from hieroglyphics; the knowledge of which was lost to the world; in which wonderful event I stood alone, an unlearned youth, to combat the worldly wisdom, and multiplied ignorance of eighteen centuries."[33] Yet the book is not an assault on learning. It calls for careful reading and celebrates the proliferation of books.[34] Moreover, its production was not a celestial magic trick meant to display divine power for its own sake. Rather, the odd miracle of its advent is a spur to soulful seeking and socializing. Through it, God reveals the limits of human learning and worldly wisdom and directs them to divine ends— not merely the pursuit of sacred knowledge and connection to an unseen world, but the reconciliation of broken families, learning from sacred histories, healing of intergenerational wounds, and the building of Zion.

Stumbling over seer stones, we might welcome the possibility that God's aim with the book involves both what it says *and* how its origin story challenges our common sense and worldly aims, even when they seem utterly reasonable and religious. Both the text and the event of the Book of Mormon call us to believe in a demanding but hopeful world wherein the way to heaven is not a path toward learned prudence or the security of wealth, but the walk of a community that puts wisdom in the service of God's call to seal ourselves together—rich and poor, ancient and modern, scholar and fool alike. ✳

1. For a brief but thorough description of the translation process, see Don Bradley, *The Lost 116 Pages: Reconstructing the Book of Mormon's Missing Stories* (Salt Lake City: Greg Kofford Books, 2019), 37–56.

2. Richard Lyman Bushman, *Joseph Smith's Gold Plates: A Cultural History* (New York: Oxford University Press, 2023), 67.

3. Bushman, *Joseph Smith's Gold Plates*, 65.

4. These lines come at the end of Smith's famous King Follett Sermon. See History, 1838–1856, volume E-1 [1 July 1843–30 April 1844], p. 1979, josephsmithpapers.org.

5. See, e.g., Patrick Q. Mason, *Planted: Belief and Belonging in an Age of Doubt* (Salt Lake City: Deseret Book, 2015), 65.

6. See, e.g., Richard Lyman Bushman, *Joseph Smith: Rough Stone Rolling* (New York: Alfred A. Knopf, 2005), 69.

7. See, e.g., "Book of Mormon Translation," Gospel Topics Essays, The Church of Jesus Christ of Latter-day Saints.

8. See, e.g., Grant Hardy, *Understanding the Book of Mormon: A Reader's Guide* (New York: Oxford University Press, 2010), xviii.

9. 1 Corinthians 1:23 (KJV, emphasis added).

10. 1 Corinthians 1:27–29 (N. T. Wright's translation, The Kingdom New Testament).

11. Samuel Morris Brown, *Joseph Smith's Translation: The Words and Worlds of Early Mormonism* (New York: Oxford University Press, 2020), 124.

12. Brown, *Joseph Smith's Translation*, 130–31.

13. Brown, *Joseph Smith's Translation*, 64.

14. Jacob 2:17.

15. See Alma 37:6 and Doctrine and Covenants 1:9–28.

16. Joseph M. Spencer, *The Vision of All: Twenty-Five Lectures on Isaiah in Nephi's Record* (Salt Lake City: Greg Kofford Books, 2016), 250.

17. 2 Nephi 27:20 (emphasis added).

18. 2 Nephi 27:25–26.

19. 2 Nephi 26:16.

20. 2 Nephi 26:20.

21. 2 Nephi 28:13.

22. 2 Nephi 29:4.

23. Isaiah 29:14 (*The Jewish Study Bible, Second Edition*).

24. Joseph Smith—History 1:28.

25. Bushman, *Joseph Smith's Gold Plates*, 13–14.

26. History, 1834–1836, 93–94, josephsmithpapers.org.

27. As Richard Bushman writes, "It may have taken four years for Joseph to purge himself of his treasure-seeking greed." *Rough Stone Rolling*, 51.

28. Bushman, *Joseph Smith's Gold Plates*, 16–17.

29. See Samuel Morris Brown, *In Heaven as It Is on Earth: Joseph Smith and the Early Mormon Conquest of Death* (New York: Oxford University Press, 2012), 81–82, 87.

30. Terryl Givens, *People of Paradox: A History of Mormon Culture* (New York: Oxford University Press, 2007), xv, 69, 74.

31. See Doctrine and Covenants 93:36 and 2 Nephi 9:28–29.

32. Grant Hardy, ed., *The Book of Mormon: A Reader's Edition* (Urbana: University of Illinois Press, 2003), 642.

33. History, 1838–1856, volume E-1 [1 July 1843–30 April 1844], p. 1775, josephsmithpapers.org.

34. 2 Nephi 29:11–14.

THE CALENDAR

Grappling with Faith at the End of Youth

AUGUST BURTON

MY LIFE AS A LATTER-DAY SAINT *has, in my mind, always been a kind of calendar.* A calendar that teaches you how to live from sunup to sundown, from Sunday to Sunday, and from year one to a time when time no longer matters. The Calendar has always been there for me. Always. As if divinely inscribed in my genetic code. But sometimes, of late, I feel like it's slipping away from me. That I am losing it.

In my earliest memories, every day starts the same. I roll out of bed and, even before I've cleared my throat, I'm in conversation with God. I wasn't the best conversation partner; I am not still. But every day started the way it should, with a plea, a laundry list of gratitude, a call home. In those early years, all my siblings started the day this same way. The younger ones—I was the youngest—spent maybe seconds on their knees in prayer. The older ones spent minutes. Perhaps they were putting in more effort. Or perhaps,

more likely, their conversations were filled with awkward pauses caused by impromptu naps, so irresistible in the first moments of morning. Regardless, once the ceremony was done, we all crisscrossed on our paths to the piano, to the kitchen, to the smaller piano, or to the bathroom. Seeing each other briefly in passing before school, we would all rejoin later in the evening for the next Calendar event.

Sometimes the next event was initiated by my father, sometimes by my mother. In any case, it was always interrupting something. But we all knew that we must come, that it was right to come, and so—sometimes easily, sometimes with resistance—we came. We came to read ancient texts lifted from golden plates and decaying parchment, now housed in a brown leather cover worn down by my mother's devoted hands. We came to hear stories, learn truth, and, if we were lucky, catch a glimpse of some too-personal insight scribbled in the margins. My mother's annotations were often meaningless to us, but other times they offered peeks into the workings of her mind, divulging things that no child could, or maybe should, understand about their mother. Every night ended in a test of willpower almost too

> These weeks built a childhood, an adolescence. They were our birthright. They were strange (and at some point we became aware that they were strange), but they were a sure foundation.

great for children that age. The challenge, of great moral significance, was to keep one's eyes shut the entire time while some preselected individual permuted stock words and phrases, sending them upward, ending the day the way it started.

Days were bookended in this manner. But days only served to create weeks. The Calendar functions on many scales, from symmetric days to unfathomable eternities, but it is the week that is its fundamental unit.

A week begins and ends on Sunday. It is a slow start and a slow finish. Once our parents had lifted us from our beds, we would fill a car and then a pew. We would spend an hour in that pew. The older children napped on adjacent shoulders while the younger children played with action figures and ate Cheerios. Anyone who could pay attention listened to that week's selection of neighbors-turned-sermon-givers and broken four-part harmonies. Finally, a tired middle-aged man would close the meeting. Then, everyone coping with their Wonder Bread breath in their own way, we were shuttled off to spend hours two and three in classes with our peers.

As a young child, hours two and three were filled with teachers desperately striving to uplift, wrangle, or simply appease their assigned menagerie of children. We spent half of the time in tiny classrooms with teachers trying to convey gospel principles through stories, scriptures, discussions, and games. We spent the other half of the time in a large common room, with leaders still trying to teach gospel principles, but this time through music and more games. These hours were chaotic, bipolar experiences. They were full of extreme hunger and excessive sugar. They were full of reverence and riotousness. They were organized and not organized enough. They were fascinating and boring. They were not all that different from life.

Exhausted from the three-hour ordeal, we would all collapse into the real work of the day—rest. Sunday naps were sacred naps, and we all participated, except for Mom, who managed nap schedules and treasured the intersection of our naps as rare time for herself. After naps, we would participate in life's most important activities. We would play catch with Dad, read books, play games, not do homework, and eat copious amounts of roast beef and gravy.

I think back and try to hear the sound of Sunday. It is silence. Organists and choirs filled our home with beautiful music that became muted by its familiarity—eventually it only registered as white noise. We spoke and we laughed, but everything in memory is blanketed by a pleasant nothingness. The absence of life's daily hassles forcefully reset the mind, sending it into the coming week as a clean slate.

Monday days were just days, but Monday evenings were public statements of priority—our family and our faith above all. Nothing interfered with Monday evenings. We opted out of practices, games, and entire teams if they attempted to stake claim to this protected time. One might expect an eleven-year-old to be resentful after having to quit his basketball team because they had signed up for a Monday-night league. On the contrary, it was deeply stabilizing to know that this family could slow the rush of life—warding off the world for a few hours to sing about popcorn, run races up the stairs in our underwear, eat chocolate-chocolate peanut butter chip cookies, and just be family. We talked about religion, sure, but the point was that our faith was family. And our family was home.

Tuesdays never made sense to me as a youth, but I suppose they were a miraculous product

Brent Croxton

of what happens when entire communities are on the Calendar. Somehow, and for some reason, parents gave up their evenings to parent someone else's teenagers. The entire neighborhood's youth population (not really, but the rest, the nonattenders, were invisible to me) would come together to be taught, entertained, and babysat by a cadre of adult volunteers. We would learn knots, go camping, play basketball, eat ice cream, rake leaves at widow so-and-so's house, and generally wonder why we were there. But we went, and it was good.

Wednesdays through Saturdays passed like a dream, full of important nonessentials. We did the school thing. The sports thing. The music, art, and whatever else thing. But these days flew by, and little was processed until things slowed down again on Sunday. The start, and the end.

These weeks built a childhood, an adolescence. They were our birthright. They were

strange (and at some point we became aware that they were strange), but they were a sure foundation. A moment of chaos, grief, or pain could strike, but in those young years, it was hard for such a moment to last. It was hard to truly suffer when you knew that in a few days you would be in a pew. The next evening at home eating cookies. The next surrounded by peers and volunteer parents. And on, and on, and on.

* * * * *

The Calendar comes with a standard set of key life events, scheduled by God, or if not God, a quorum of twelve men whose collective age and wisdom surely sums to that of most deities. For Children of the Calendar, the majority of events

Brent Croxton

occur at fixed points, early in life. They come at eight, twelve, fourteen, sixteen, and eighteen years of age. Each comes at a formative moment. Each is an opportunity to deepen one's commitment to a community that transcends time but not place. During each, covenants are made horizontally and vertically, building out the structure of the cosmos. When I was eight, I accepted the invitation to the first event and, in so doing, committed my rather sober mind to timeliness. I would be prepared for each event, at the right time. I would be who the Calendar was designed to make me.

By junior high, I had mastered the Calendar. I did not fully grasp its significance, but this did not hinder a near-perfect performance. I began adding to it. Now, every Thursday morning before sunrise, I would pay a visit to the temple perched on the mountain overlooking my home. In the dark, the temple is uplit and visible for miles across the valley. A golden angel Moroni balances atop the sharp central spire that rises from the glowing white stone—he beckons, calling me into the Lord's home. I ascend the mountain and enter. His house is staffed by elderly Saints, draped in white. They shuffle through granite halls, whispering. When I arrive, they are not surprised that I am accompanied by ghosts—ancestral ghosts, long deceased relatives awakened by my diligent internet sleuthing, stirred by a child's remembrance of

their lives. I am guided to the edge of a large basin, held on the backs of twelve stone oxen. The warm baptismal water hugs me as I descend. My spirits, my family of generations past, watch from the edge of the basin. They vibrate at a low frequency as they hear their names read aloud, producing a deep hum that doesn't quite pierce the veil but reverberates inside of me. They witness as I am submerged in the water, and then, with grateful hands, they lift me gently out, dripping. Thirty minutes later and still trailing threads of eternity, I descend the mountain, enter the earthy brick structure of Corner Canyon High School, and sit down to learn the quadratic formula. Surrounded by mortals again.

Through junior high, the Calendar was almost exclusively a source of harmony in my life. It was simple and authoritative. It provided a clear, glowing vision for my life this week, next year, this life, and the endless time after that. By this age, I understood and embraced the person that the Calendar was going to make me, the person that my eight-year-old self had committed to becoming. I knew each necessary step along the path and when it would happen. I derived profound comfort in a good life mapped out, start to nonexistent end.

High school brought challenges to life within the Calendar. Initial difficulties were purely logistical. At this point, I was somewhat experienced with, and probably addicted to, meeting and exceeding others' expectations. Determined to shine, I approached my academics and athletics with zeal. They soaked up my time like a sponge, and the first victims were those incomprehensible Tuesday evenings. Life was full of deadlines and commitments, and I couldn't justify spending the hour with volunteer parents and increasingly unenthusiastic youth. These absences were of no practical significance; but they symbolized an encroachment. This was some foreign, uninspired calendar forcing its way in. I say forcing, but I allowed it, giving way to the perceived pressures of life.

At the same time scheduling pressure was building, I began to encounter difficulties with something even more foundational than the Calendar. In my head, there exists a set of

> **I knew I couldn't sweep away the dust of those shattered truths. I knew that if I searched through that dust on hands and knees, mostly knees, I would find specks of gold.**

spiritual truths. Many have been gifted to me by my parents or faith community, while others have been earned through experience. These truths are as fundamental to the order of my inner life as chemical bonds are to the order of nature. They bind together all my disparate, lived experiences into a coherent narrative and point me in the direction of a meaningful life. Throughout high school, many of these truths revealed themselves to be brittle. During these dramatic years, I was confronted with a series of bitter ironies. Things that shouldn't have been true, couldn't have been true, and yet were true, stared me in the face. Prophets speak for God, and yet prophets can be wrong, horribly wrong. Heavenly Mother is a deity coequal with Heavenly Father, and yet earthly mothers are conferred no religious power or authority that is unmediated by earthly men. God loves all Their children, and yet God supposedly only works amongst the seventeen million of them around the globe who fortuitously found their way into this American church. Slowly at first, and then with shocking rapidity, many of the bonds of my inner life shattered into dust. Each loss caused my stomach to drop. It was as if I were in a prolonged fall at the end of a dream. Without these truths, the Calendar could not be justified. Without the Calendar, I would be lost in time.

I wandered alone through crowded high school halls, staring with vacant eyes into a world that I once saw clearly but was now fading into a cold, empty black. I strained my eyes, searching for glimmers of light. I went through the motions of taking tests, submitting papers, and sitting through class, hoping that in those haunted, hallowed walks from chemistry to history, I would come to understand something of actual import. I would rediscover some familiar truth. I would find something with which to rebuild.

Why did I exert my mind, mining for material with which to rebuild? Why did I stare past the vibrant faces of my peers and into the vast emptiness of a receding world? Why did I ignore the teeming life around me, instead searching for signs of life in another realm? Because I knew. I knew I couldn't sweep away the dust of those shattered truths. I knew that if I searched through that dust on hands and knees, mostly knees, I would find specks of gold.

And I did. I found softer truths, of similar form but holier function, to replace the hard truths that had crashed against the rock of reality. I began forming new bonds, cautiously. I packaged the truths I found with a measured dose of uncertainty, infusing each new bond with some much-needed elasticity. Prophets can be inspired to speak for God, and whenever they do, they do so imperfectly because they are imperfect. Heavenly Mother is a deity coequal with Heavenly Father, and earthly mothers lack religious power and authority because of the near-universal sickness of patriarchy and not because of divine will. God loves all Their children, and this no-longer American church is one important tool for making that love accessible to all. At times, the process felt like building a sandcastle at the bottom of the ocean. Hopeless, too much pressure. But when I found a spiritual truth, a truth that was resilient, it was electric. My soul would sing, my previously vacant eyes would brim with directionless love, and then I would continue. I continued the search, and by the end of high school, I had rebuilt my inner life. Not every bond in the original structure was added back, but I had rebuilt it enough to save the Calendar from free fall. My vision through time, of my future, was a bit cloudier now that the Calendar was supported by ambiguity. But the clouds were nonthreatening. Their very presence was a reminder that they were part of a larger landscape.

Nevertheless, the crush of academic and other pressures continued to be a threat to the Calendar, and so the end of high school and the start of the next event couldn't come soon enough. The next event was a Latter-day Saint mission, a respite from regular life but itself the furthest thing from respite. It was an all-consuming, unceasing event that lasted from age eighteen to age twenty—a perfect tithe on life. It is the institution's most concerted attempt to sear the Calendar into the hearts of the rising generation. I found myself suddenly living in the most southern tip of Texas, in a valley with no mountains, new language in tow, grinding through the most confounding experience of my life. These years cannot be explained. How does one explain being nineteen and the ecclesiastical leader of a congregation composed solely of ex-gangsters? How does one explain the thrill of being a teacher, janitor, spiritual guide, landscaper, marriage counselor, pseudo-exorcist, therapist . . . and the simultaneous pain of being nothing at all? How does one explain the joy of committing oneself completely to the wellbeing of others, and the agony of not always doing it for the right reasons? One does not. Some say these were the best two years of their lives. Others say they were the worst two years. Still others say they were the best two years *for* their lives. They are all lying. Secretly, they are still processing. They will always be processing.

One of the great ironies of these two years is that while we (myself and an assigned companion) were busy onboarding newcomers to the Calendar, we ourselves were living a much more regimented and wholly unsustainable version of it. The daily schedule is tattooed into my mind: Wake up at 6:30 a.m. Pray. Exercise for a half hour, eat for a half hour, get ready for a half hour. Pray. Study for an hour. Pray. Plan your work for every half hour remaining in the day, for a half hour. Pray. Pretend to be an extrovert for two hours while attempting to talk to people who want nothing to do with you. Lunch. Learn a new language for an hour. Pray. Leave the apartment until ten o'clock at night, serving and teaching and facing a lifetime's worth of rejection. Be the blessed beneficiaries of the greatest generosity

and the cursed collectors of the vilest vitriol. Come home. Collapse. Pray.

In retrospect, I was fortunate to spend almost 180 of these taxing days in Sinton. Sinton is a blip of a town smooshed between fields of cotton, with a population of stray dogs that rivals that of the humans. There is a main street with a dollar store at each end. There is a church where the Mexicans used to go and a church where the whites used to go. There is an equal number of family-run auto shops and family-run restaurants. And there is a symmetric smattering of houses on either side of the town's equator. Time here was measured in conversations with neighbors, in Friday-night football games, and in annual agriculture shows. Not in half hours. It was uncomfortable to try and force our fast-paced, minutely planned schedules onto a place where time hardly existed, and so we slowed a little. We tried to focus on what really matters, like pristine front lawns. For three months, we dragged a green metal wagon through the streets, borrowed garden tools clanking in the back, and offered our hands. At Christmas, we adorned the wagon with lights.

Through this and other means, we met a small collection of beautiful souls who made the Calendar their own. They lived it authentically, in individualized ways, informed by their diverse lives. There was the Moreno family. They had quit street life some years back when they first started living the Calendar, but the swanky style and family-first attitude of the gangs never left. The dad was a short, heavyset man with a walrus mustache and a debilitating limp. When he would heave himself up by his cane into his massive, siren-red F-150, all that was visible through the windshield was the glint of the large silver rings that adorned his right hand, resting atop the steering wheel. Everyone else in the family drove classic cars they customized themselves. On Sundays after church, the family cruised slowly through the streets, parade style, trunks open, blasting bass so deep that the doors of half the town rattled in their frames. Somehow they lived the Calendar without an extensive supporting community or hierarchical oversight. Their relaxed, family-above-all approach was

Brent Croxton

protective. Despite their difficult lives, the greatest tragedy they reported was when their jeweler two towns over, who provided them with their thick gold chains and dazzling diamond studs, was shot dead by his jealous elderly father.

There was also Jeff. When I first met Jeff, he was sitting on the step of his porch, streams of vape swirling violently around his unruly beard and shiny bald head, his shirtless torso a mural of anime characters inked onto a pale, freckled canvas. He looked like a dragon, and he was a dragon, of sorts. He was a single father with a knack for nurturing, keeper of the light in his young daughters' eyes. The Calendar can be overwhelming for parents without a partner, but Jeff, seeing the spark it brought his girls, determinedly came home from long days of work in the sewers to guide his family through the ropes of the Calendar.

There were others. A broken family piecing themselves back together and giving each other grace. A young man buzzing on six hundred milligrams of daily caffeine, looking for a stable pattern for life before heading off to boot camp. They were all living proof that the Calendar could be lived in different ways, and different was good.

At the end of those Texan years, I stumbled off the plane and into the rest of life. I was beyond weary.

The last two years had been in turn dizzying, traumatic, exhilarating, and exhaustingly meaningful. And yet, upon seeing my family for the first time in two years (and the first time all together in six), I felt lighter than ever. A staggering weight of responsibility had been lifted from my shoulders, and I was excited to live *my* life again. The only problem was, I came home an adult.

The Calendar exists for adults, but it's different from the one I lived growing up. It is centered around re-creating the Calendar for your children, passing on the birthright. I don't have children. In fact, most of my time is spent outside the secure bounds of a formal family structure. Even when I go home—*home* home, the home I grew up in—it is not the same as before. It is not the same, and not just because we're almost all adults now.

At some point in the blur of those two mission years, I got a call from my oldest sister, announcing her resignation from the Calendar. I know it was a Monday, because Monday was the day we could talk to family. A few years after that, my oldest brother quietly followed suit. Growing up, we always had two fundamental things in common: blood and the Calendar. Now, it's down to blood. At Thanksgiving, Christmas, or any other time we might all be home, there is joy, lots of joy, but there is also a discomfort, a loss. Days now start in myriad ways. The evening event still happens, but discreetly. Not everyone receives the call to gather. All are welcome, but the event is advertised via text and, out of respect, only to those still on the Calendar. Instead of gathering around the ottoman in the family room, we

Now, as an adult with an all-too-rational mind, trained in the brutal practice of deconstruction, there is too often a disquieting distance between God and Me. The awful space provided by this separation allows Me to analyze God and choose who God is. Whether God is. And whether God will continue along with Me.

gather in someone's bedroom. This preserves the center of the home as a neutral space.

Sundays now begin with separation. Some go and others do not. Each is presumably happy with their choice; everyone would be happier had choices aligned. The experience for those who fill our now smaller pew is altered. Shoulders have a different function now. While they were once for naps, they are now a metric for how the meeting is going. If my mom's shoulders are relaxed, I know to look for tears. Tears mean her heart is touched, not wounded. If my mom's shoulders are tense, I know something has gone terribly wrong. Occasionally when this happens, she and I will discuss the offending topic when we get home. Other times, she instead recedes to her room, and, later that evening, I will receive a text. She will apologize for whatever negative verbal reaction she let escape, typically nothing more than a terse critique. I require no apology; I felt it too.

When a visit home comes to an end and the adult siblings return to their lives scattered across the country, there is sadness. We will miss each other. But there is, I think, a regrettable and unspoken sense of relief. On your own, you can live according to whatever calendar you like without being confronted by the sorrow of time experienced differently.

Back on my own, I struggle to preserve the Calendar. Some of the challenges are, once again, logistical. In my chosen path, I stare far more at screens than I do at eternities. On Sunday afternoons there is no playing catch with Dad, only catching up. Catching up on an amount of work that could not possibly be contained within the "work" week. There is hardly time for humans, let alone spirits and gods. But this is superficial. The greater threat is me.

My thoughts are too much my own. When I was younger, two entities existed in my mind. God and Me, but there was no clear distinction between the two. One melded into the other, so many of my thoughts were laced with wisdom from another world, a world unseen but more pure and more real. Now, as an adult with an all-too-rational mind, trained in the brutal practice of deconstruction, there is too often a disquieting distance between God and Me. The awful space provided by this separation allows Me to analyze God and choose who God is. Whether God is. And whether God will continue along with Me. I feel the burden of living by intention rather than Godly intuition, and I am weary. I feel like it's slipping away from me. That I am losing it.

And yet, even in my weariness, I cannot deny the seemingly stochastic infusions of goodness into my life. A friendship so profoundly good that it could not have been made, only given. The subtle iridescence tingeing memories of my past. Strange waves of peace during chaotic times. Comforting moments of synchronicity. These are small rays of light piercing an ostensibly closed system—bursts of energy that keep spiritual entropy at bay. Sometimes these unscheduled interventions make me wonder. And wonder is enough. Sometimes they leave me with hope. And hope is enough. Sometimes they leave me in awe. And awe is enough. Perhaps one day wonder, hope, and awe will coalesce into something so concrete as the Calendar. But for now, this is enough. ✳

BOOK REVIEW
BENJAMIN PARK'S *AMERICAN ZION*
ILLUSTRATED AND WRITTEN BY LOGAN MICKEL

THE ETERNITY MIRROR.

IT'S ONE OF OUR FAVORITE OBJECT LESSONS IN MORMONDOM,

RIGHT UP THERE WITH THE GLOVE/HAND SPIRIT SHTICK AND COMPARING THE HOLY GHOST TO THE FORCE IN STAR WARS.

STAND BETWEEN TWO MIRRORS AND YOU'LL CATCH A GLIMPSE OF ETERNITY, BOTH THE FUTURE AND EVERY GENERATION OF THE PAST WHOSE CHOICES INFLUENCED THE PRESENT, GENERATION, AFTER GENERATION, AFTER GENERATION AFTER GENERATION AFTER GENERATION AFTER GENERATION AFTER GENERATION AFTER

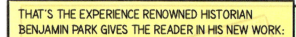

THAT'S THE EXPERIENCE RENOWNED HISTORIAN BENJAMIN PARK GIVES THE READER IN HIS NEW WORK:

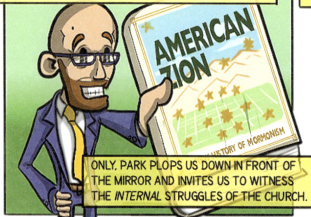

ONLY, PARK PLOPS US DOWN IN FRONT OF THE MIRROR AND INVITES US TO WITNESS THE *INTERNAL* STRUGGLES OF THE CHURCH.

USING NEWLY AVAILABLE SOURCES, PARK SHINES A LIGHT ON THE DEBATES AND ARGUMENTS FROM *WITHIN* THAT SHAPED THE FAITH AND LED TO WHERE WE ARE TODAY.

AMERICAN ZION IS REPLETE WITH EXAMPLES.

FOR INSTANCE...

HYMN OF THE ALLOPARENT

JEANINE
BEE

I RECENTLY LEARNED THAT MY TWO-year-old son calls his nursery leaders "Mama" and "Dada." My son is not one of those toddlers who colors quietly during church. Instead, on this particular Sabbath, he had decided to be an especially noisy allosaurus during the sacrament, so I took him out into the foyer. I held him in my arms as he squirmed and wiggled and whined, trying to get free so that he could burst back into the chapel. At that moment, his nursery leaders walked in the door. My son saw them and immediately cried out, "Mama, help! Dada, help!"

In hindsight, viewed from a distance, it was a humorous exchange. But in the midst of the experience, all I felt was guilt. Like my son's call for help meant that I wasn't living up to the heavy responsibilities of motherhood. All of my inadequacies as a parent flashed through my brain in rapid succession: all the times I felt annoyed at my children's unending requests, or I didn't sit on the floor to play or read with them. The times when I raised my voice or made empty threats because it was easier than connecting with them in a difficult moment. The times I lost my patience or my temper. As my son reached out to his dear nursery leaders, all I could think was, *Am I so insufficient as his mother that someone else could so easily take my place?*

Of course, this kind of "mom guilt" is not unique; parents all over the world worry about doing what is best for their children. But I feel as if I also had another layer of guilt, this one connected to my religious upbringing. Being raised in The Church of Jesus Christ of Latter-day Saints, I had heard so many talks and lessons about the importance of the nuclear family and motherhood in particular. "None other can adequately take her place."[1] And now here was my child, calling out for another woman to be his mother. Of course, I also understood that these depths of meaning cannot be attributed to a toddler whose current method of communication is mainly

growling like a dinosaur, so I tucked away my discomfort and sent my son to nursery. A few days later, still a little raw from that experience, I discovered the idea of an "alloparent," and I understood that what had felt like my son replacing me as a parent was actually him finding support in ways that both nature and God intended. In that moment of frustration, an alloparent was exactly what my little allosaurus needed.

An alloparent is someone in a community who helps raise a child that is not their direct offspring. Some examples of alloparents can include church leaders, grandparents, stepparents, neighbors, aunts, uncles, schoolteachers, cousins, family friends, even siblings or stepsiblings. I was introduced to the term in the book *Hunt, Gather, Parent* by Michaeleen Doucleff. The book is a collection of parenting lessons that Doucleff gathered as she visited with traditional cultures all over the world—specifically, the centuries-old child-rearing methods of the Maya people, the Inuit people, and the hunter-gatherer societies that still exist today. I sought additional information about the anthropological understanding of alloparents in the book *Mothers and Others: The Evolutionary Origins of Mutual Understanding* by anthropologist Sarah Hrdy. Both Doucleff and Hrdy explore alloparenting mainly in the context of hunter-gatherer communities. But as I read these two books and learned more about alloparenting, it all felt comfortable, even familiar to me. I realized that, while alloparenting may not be a strong norm in Western society as a whole, alloparents are actually very important in the doctrine and culture of The Church of Jesus Christ of Latter-day Saints.

With hymns like "Families Can Be Together Forever" and "Love at Home," lessons for children and youth celebrating temple marriage, and countless conference talks about the weighty responsibilities of mothers and fathers, it sometimes feels as if a majority of the Church's

teachings revolve around the importance of the traditional nuclear family unit. But, while the nuclear family is absolutely important to both the Church and our society today, most scholars characterize the exclusive focus on the nuclear family as a shift that only occurred within the last century.[2] Prior to the nuclear family template, human society established and defined families in a slightly different way. Vestiges of this societal organization can be seen in the structure and traditions of ancient and contemporary tribal communities. For example, in the Nayaka hunter-gatherer tribes in southern India, "adults call all the children around their home 'son' or 'daughter'. . . and all the older people in their community 'little father,' . . . and 'little mother.'"[3] Church members might recognize this tradition as similar to one of our own: calling each other "brother" and "sister."

We are blessed in our faith tradition to have an understanding of families that spreads so much farther and goes so much deeper than just the nuclear family unit. We believe in a family that can be sealed together for eternity, through countless generations, from child to parent to grandparent. It's a family unit that is just as important and serves just as many purposes as the modern nuclear family. The branches of this eternal family tree spread wide enough to encompass siblings and cousins and aunts and uncles. Even when loved ones have passed from this life, we have the power to graft them onto our living tree through posthumous temple work. And, if you dig down far enough, you'd find that we all spring from the same roots. You. Me. Your neighbor. A stranger on the other side of the planet. Across distance and time, we share both the same heavenly parents and the same physical ancestors. We call each other "brother" and "sister" for good reason.

This Latter-day Saint tradition holds multiple levels of doctrinal meaning for us; it comes from our knowledge about the family and our unique beliefs about God's sealing power. It also speaks to the existence of a religious family, one into which we are "adopted" when we take upon ourselves baptismal covenants and agree to bear one another's burdens. But while our tradition of calling each other "brother" and "sister" was born of ancient knowledge that was restored

Across distance and time, we share both the same heavenly parents and the same physical ancestors. We call each other "brother" and "sister" for good reason.

through modern revelation, the Nayaka practice comes from ancient knowledge that was never lost. They call each other family because they treat each other as family. Every child is provided for and cared for by every adult. Every elder provides wisdom and nurturing to those who need it. The group works together to raise strong, healthy children who share their societal values.

In the social sciences, it has been theorized that this kind of alloparenting was necessary for the success of the human race. Human children are born so much more helpless than other species and stay helpless for so much longer than any other species. In ancient hunter-gatherer societies, it would have been prohibitively challenging for a mother and father alone to provide all of the attention, protection, and calories that a baby needed to survive. Alloparents would have vastly improved the chances of keeping children alive in an unforgiving, prehistoric setting. Today, parents rely on complex economic systems to provide for their children materially. Feeding a child involves supply chains that stretch around the world, sustained by too many workers for us to ever meet and thank. But our economic systems are not as effective at providing emotional relationships, and research suggests children do better developmentally when alloparents are directly involved in their care. One study found that, in a Gusii village in Kenya, "even though a Gusii child's nutritional status was best predicted by the security of his attachment to his mother . . . the strongest predictor of empathy, dominance, independence, and achievement orientation often turned out to be a strong attachment to a nonparental caretaker."[4] And a series of studies conducted in Israel and the Netherlands found that "overall, children seemed to do best [socioemotionally] when they have three secure relationships—that is, three relationships that send the clear message, 'you will be cared for no matter what.'"[5]

Within The Church of Jesus Christ of Latter-day Saints, so much time and so many resources are dedicated to teaching and raising other people's children. In fact, in 2019, some of the bishop's responsibilities were shifted to the Relief Society president and elders quorum president because, in President Russell M. Nelson's words, the bishop's "first and foremost responsibility is to care for the young men and young women of his ward."[6] The alloparenting done within the walls of a meetinghouse can have resounding benefits for the children, families, and alloparents involved. As newlyweds living in Northern Virginia, my husband and I served as Sunbeam teachers. For two hours every Sunday, we had the opportunity to teach those little boys valuable lessons, like "Jesus loves you" and "You are the boss of your own body (We don't kiss our friends at church)." We taught them Primary songs, fed them Goldfish and mini marshmallows, and reminded them to flush and wash their hands after they used the bathroom. And all week long, we loved them. They weren't our children, but they were "our kids," and our involvement with them expanded our hearts and enriched our lives. The experiences that we had serving as alloparents to those Sunbeams would even help us as we started parenting our own children. Years later, when I learned that my five-year-old son had been sent to the principal's office for chasing down his friends at recess to give them kisses, I could have panicked. *Where did he learn this? This can't be normal. Do we need a child psychologist?* But thanks to my experiences with those three-year-old boys, I not only had a lens of "normal childhood behavior" with which to compare my son, but I already had a "we don't kiss our friends" speech ready to go.

Of course, that's not to say that one needs a calling to participate in alloparenting. Primary General President Sister Dwan J. Young taught, "We are all teachers of children—parents, aunts, uncles, grandparents, priesthood leaders, ward members, neighbors. Children are always

Brooke Bowen

watching and learning. We teach them through our behavior as well as by what we say. They watch how we treat each other. They listen to the voices of their parents and to the voices at church."[7] As a ward organist, I take the sacrament on the stand every other week, leaving my husband to corral our four children in the pews. On one such week, I heard the shriek of my allosaurus/toddler as my husband carried him out of the chapel, leaving our three older kids sitting on their own. The fighting began just as soon as the sacrament prayer ended. I felt my jaw clench as my daughters' bickering disturbed the quiet reverence of the chapel. I started to calculate which would be a greater interruption to the meeting: me rushing down from the stand in the middle of the sacrament, or the imminent name-calling and subsequent tears. But before I could land on a decision, my neighbor and friend (who also happens to know my children as one of their elementary school teachers) quietly shifted to their pew. She held my youngest daughter on her lap and whispered kindly in her ear. My life is peppered with tender moments like this, in and out of my church experience. My brother rocking my newborn baby to sleep. The next-door neighbor inviting my kids over for homemade ice cream. A second-grade teacher wiping frustrated tears from my son's cheeks. I never feel so loved as when I see others loving my children.

Brooke Bowen

Studies have shown that alloparenting benefits children, nuclear families, and even the alloparents themselves, but perhaps the greatest benefit of alloparenting can be seen in human society. When a mother hands her child over to a teacher, grandparent, cousin, neighbor, sibling, or babysitter, she is manifesting a society built on trust. Evolutionarily speaking, she has to be reasonably confident that the person holding her baby will care for them, feed them, and protect them from danger. She has to believe that human society is dependable and that the world is well intentioned. By extending this kind of trust to the world around her, a mother creates a large family system for her child, which the child, in turn, learns to trust. It's a difficult ask for me—I'm the kind of mom who likes to feel "in control." Letting my children develop healthy relationships with other adults means giving up some of that control. It means letting my kids learn that "different" isn't necessarily "wrong." And alloparents must do their part to create a system built on trust, as well. When acting as an alloparent, we need to *be* trustworthy—develop relationships with the parents of the children we care for; participate in and abide by the rules outlined in youth protection trainings; support those who come forward as victims of abuse. These kinds of measures can not only protect children and families

from harm, but can also protect the sacred trust required to sustain an alloparenting society.

However, this trust can also be fragile, and today's Western culture seems to be pushing society in the opposite direction, engendering distrust in the world by separating us from each other. In Hrdy's words, "The modern emphasis on individualism and personal independence along with consumption-oriented economies, compartmentalized living arrangements in highrise apartments or suburban homes, and neo-local residence patterns combine to undermine social connectedness."[8] As this feeling of disconnect increases, as we turn inwards to focus on our nuclear families while excluding a potential social network of alloparents, we teach our children that the world cannot be trusted. And, perhaps more significantly, "a subset of children today [will] grow up and survive to adulthood without ever forging trusting relationships with caring adults, and their childhood experiences are likely to be predictive of how they in turn will take care of others."[9] Children who do not know how to trust the world will grow and raise their own children in that same distrustful environment. Indeed, as the Family Proclamation declares, the eternal family is "the fundamental unit of society."[10] And as generations of humans forget how to trust and care for their eternal spirit brothers and sisters, society will crumble as "compassion and the quest for emotional connection . . . fade away."[11]

We are accustomed to thinking of The Church of Jesus Christ of Latter-day Saints as the home of the restored gospel; nearly every fast and testimony meeting, someone stands up and expresses their gratitude for and faith in the restored gospel of Jesus Christ. But it is important to remember, in this world of increasing division and individualism, that the Church is also the home of the restored family—an ancient, eternal, all-encompassing family, where the needs of a single child are met by a village of loving alloparents. The practice of alloparenting is even modeled by our Heavenly Father, as President Gordon B. Hinckley reminds us. "Never forget," he said, "that these little ones are the sons and daughters of God and that yours is a custodial relationship to them, that He was a parent before you were parents and that He has not relinquished His parental rights or interest in these His little ones."[12] Following our Heavenly Father's example in this situation requires sometimes stepping back as a parent—not relinquishing our parental rights and obligations, but allowing our children to make healthy, loving connections with their nursery leaders, aunts and uncles, or friends' parents. It means building trusting relationships with your neighborhood librarian, your child's schoolteacher, or your elderly neighbor. It means understanding that your child and your family might need something that it can't manufacture from within. And it means functioning as an alloparent to children outside of your nuclear family unit, as well. In the wise words of Subion, a Hadzabe mother in Tanzania, "Ultimately, you are responsible for your own children, but you have to love all the children like your own."[13] I'll admit that sometimes it's difficult as a parent to step back and watch the young, newlywed Primary teachers fumble as they try their best to teach my children. And there are also times when it's hard for me to participate as an alloparent—to step in as a neighbor or aunt or church leader when it already feels like my job as a mother takes so much from me mentally, emotionally, and physically. But that's the beauty of our ancient, eternal, human family. We've always needed each other.

The task of parenting doesn't feel so herculean when I see so many shoulders around me ready to help with the yoke. And when my burden feels a little lighter, it gives me the opportunity to look around and see who might need an extra set of hands in their pew.

Historian Stephanie Coontz noted, "Children do best in societies where childrearing is considered too important to be left entirely to parents."[14] I consider The Church of Jesus Christ of Latter-day Saints to be one of these societies. In fact, James E. Faust said of child-rearing, "To me, there is no more important human effort."[15] We weren't meant to go through life alone. And we weren't meant to parent alone, either. We need partners in our efforts—in the Church, in our neighborhoods, and in our communities. And we need to be that support to others as well. Because it is only with this kind of selfless love and familial trust pollinating the branches of our eternal family tree that human society can flourish. ✳

1. Gordon B. Hinckley, "Women of the Church," *Ensign*, November 1996, 69.

2. Sarah Blaffer Hrdy, *Mothers and Others: The Evolutionary Origins of Mutual Understanding* (Cambridge: Harvard University Press, 2009), 144.

3. Michaeleen Doucleff, *Hunt, Gather, Parent: What Ancient Cultures Can Teach Us about the Lost Art of Raising Happy, Helpful Little Humans* (New York: Avid Reader Press, 2021), 280.

4. Hrdy, *Mothers and Others*, 131.

5. Hrdy, *Mothers and Others*, 129.

6. Russell M. Nelson, "Witnesses, Aaronic Priesthood Quorums, and Young Women Classes," *Ensign*, November 2019, 39.

7. Dwan J. Young, "Teach Children the Gospel," *Ensign*, May 1988, 78.

8. Hrdy, *Mothers and Others*, 286.

9. Hrdy, *Mothers and Others*, 291.

10. "The Family: A Proclamation to the World," General Relief Society Meeting, September 23, 1995.

11. Hrdy, *Mothers and Others*, 293.

12. "Messages of Inspiration from President Hinckley," *Church News*, March 1, 1997, 2.

13. Doucleff, *Hunt, Gather, Parent*, 281.

14. Quoted in Hrdy, *Mothers and Others*, 103.

15. James E. Faust, "The Greatest Challenge in the World—Good Parenting," *Ensign*, November 1990, 32.

OUR SAVIOR WENT WHERE NO ONE'S GONE

JOHN DURHAM PETERS
& ETHAN F. WICKMAN

Words & Music
John Durham Peters (b. 1958)
Ethan F. Wickman (b. 1973)

To listen to a recording of this hymn, visit
wayfare.org/our-savior-went.

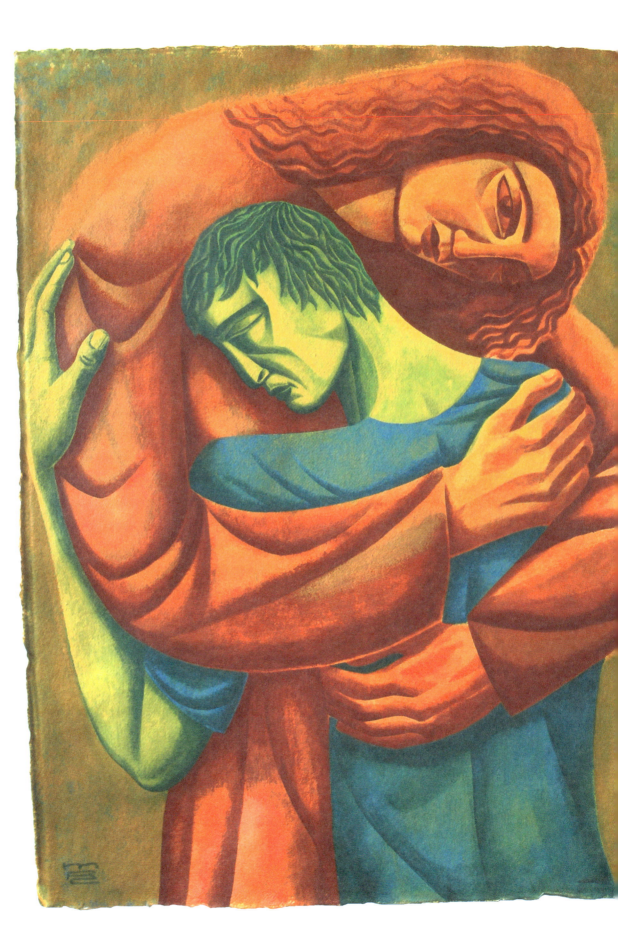

TWO TRIPS UP THE MOUNTAIN

Transactional Law & the Law of Love

STEVE YOUNG

IN MY WALK WITH GOD, I FIND THE law of love to be quite simple: loving others as God loves them, seeking their healing, expecting nothing in return. In sports, business, church, politics, at home—the fundamentals of the Restoration apply: Heavenly Parents, the fact that we are all divine and we're here together to learn and grow, and that Christ came to save and to heal. But the way we use those fundamentals to chew on the issues of life often ends up being transactional.

So much of what we do is in transaction. I often think about Moses's two trips up the mountain. The first trip up the mountain, God gave him the higher, holier work: the law of healing, which is really the law of love. The selfless act of loving is the higher, holier way. Moses took it down to the camp of Israel, and then he saw what was going on with Aaron and the golden calf. Moses said to himself, *I don't think this is going to work.* And so he went back up the mountain.

I appreciate that second trip up the mountain, because God gave Moses the transactional law, thinking, *We've got to start somewhere.* God wants a relationship with us. When God saw what was going on with the Israelites, God thought, *I know*

the experience of humanity, and I know that they're in an entropic environment, where everything rots and decays. Let's try something that is more intuitive. Let them do things for credit. Let them do things that make them feel special.

God's intention in revealing the law was to build a relationship with us, because God wants us close. God wants intimacy with us. So on the second trip up the mountain, God gave Moses a set of things to do that would build a sacred transactional relationship.

But at its root, transaction can't last in this entropic world where everything decays. That's why Moses's second trip brought back a preparatory, transactional law. We love transaction because we love feeling special. If I'm going to sacrifice in a high-demand religion that asks so much of me, human nature says, well, then I want credit. Tell me it's for a purpose, even if it's a heavenly purpose.

I spent my early years doing homework listening to *Saturday's Warrior.*[1] I found great meaning in that principle: the idea that I was here on God's errand, and I was important and useful and I could be special. A lot of my life was spent doing things to earn that moniker of being a Saturday's

> **Then Paul said, in effect, there's no way all these rules are flowing from God's love. They're actually distracting us from God's love because we view them as transactions with a distant God who is easily offended by sin and must be appeased.**

warrior. It was a great profit for me, and I was very grateful. It defined my spiritual life. I think that that's true for so many of us: we want to do good. Like, *God, tell me what to do, and I'll have it done by 10 a.m., and I'll have a Jell-O pudding pie ready to go by noon. I can do it.* We are the can-do people. And so we take Moses's second trip up the mountain with him: God telling us what to do and we do it, in a sacred relationship.

I don't want to diminish that relationship. It's just that the relationship can't last, because it's about me. That relationship is self-interested at its root, and self-interest rots over time. In the specialness of it, the accomplishment, we separate from others, because if I'm a Saturday's warrior, well, sorry, maybe you're not. So God is asking for a relationship that God knows can't last, but wants it as a beginning that is intuitive to us.

As we have taken that second trip up the mountain with Moses and come back with a transactional law, we have made it our religion, which I do not believe was the intent. I think Christ came to fulfill that law. A good friend recently wrote to me that the law of Moses became 613 laws that actually served to corrupt the practice of their religion. Look what this law paradigm did. Paul lived it fully, but it made him small and judgmental and angry. His encounter with Jesus changed everything because it introduced him to God's love. Then Paul said, in effect, there's no way all these rules are flowing from God's love. They're actually distracting us from

God's love because we view them as transactions with a distant God who is easily offended by sin and must be appeased.

I think it's important that we recognize that both trips up the mountain by Moses have different paradigms, different languages, and different actions. We see that in scripture. I can read scripture and say, *That's a transactional scripture.* It's still scripture, but it comes from the paradigm of Moses's second trip up the mountain. Or, conversely, *There is a nontransactional scripture.* That one will last. That one can make it through eternity.

So we ask ourselves, how much of my relationship with heaven is based on a transactional relationship? I was with my stake president one day when we were talking about this, and he stopped and thought about it. He said, "You know, sadly, I think most of my relationship with heaven is transactional, and it doesn't feel good."

I think that's an important vulnerability, recognizing that we don't have it all figured out. It's highly complex, as it's meant to be. We need to be vulnerable enough to see when we've messed up and made a mistake.

What would I tell my kids if I could have them learn one thing in life? It is to have that sacred round of forgiveness. If they've made a mistake, apologize, and then go fix it. And in that selfless effort to go fix it is the irony of our lives, because in that is the full measure of heaven.

In considering transactional relationships rotting over time in self-interest, I wonder, what is the far end of transactional relationships? They take us to fundamentalism and perfectionism—things that can be very, very dastardly. With that in mind, we recognize that we cannot travel that road forever. But we can begin by using it to build a relationship, starting with the transactional idea that if I'm perfect, God will bless me with abundance. That sacred transactional relationship with God results in intimacy, proximity, and a measure of spirit—all beautiful, wonderful things that lead us past transaction and deeper into a relationship with heaven.

In church, you can start to see how the water can be muddied by transaction. You hear talks that are very transactional, and you hear talks that are very nontransactional. It's important for all of us to recognize the difference between Moses's two trips up the mountain. I can be grateful for both by putting them in their proper place. As I mentioned, self-interest cannot stand forever. I firmly believe that there are perpetual places in the universe, governed by a perpetual law, which cannot be a law of transaction.

Now we need to mature into a higher, holier work. It starts by recognizing that in the *doing*, we're not getting to the places we want to be. It's not the *doing*, but the *being*: living the four qualities of long-suffering, gentle persuasion, meekness, and love unfeigned.

Someone in my Sunday School class said, "Well, then what do we do? Because we're the can-do people, right? Like, how do I do it?" And I said, "Well, actually, there's not anything to *do*. There's just things to *be*." And in the *being* is where the magic of the ironies of God's love are. I started to *be* these four qualities in my relationships at home, at work, on the street. If I was going to speak the language of long-suffering, what would that language be? If I was going to act in a way that was gentle persuasion, what would that look like?

Through meekness, the ability to be vulnerable, and the promise of Moroni 7 (the pure love of Christ), we can actually see other human beings with transfigured eyesight and see their eternal potential. Not in the moment of today, with the choices they have made in this crazy world, but

Michael Cook

their eternal potential. That is the higher, holier work of Moses's first trip up the mountain and for the thousands of years since.

I think God has asked us to leave behind a transactional relationship with Him and with Her, and to move forward in a relationship guided by this principle of eternal love. You can't conflate the two paradigms. The law of love is supreme, and then all other laws of God come as an invitation, because there is no coercion in the gospel of Jesus Christ. Christ's outstretched hands are always eternally inviting forward. In that *being*, we can transition to changing the world.

It is a selfless act to try to see another human in their fullness, their beauty, their faith to take a body to come to this earth, in the divinity of all of us together, seeking others' healing as we bounce around together, and losing ourselves in that effort. Because "God is love." And in that love, we can see others and we can heal.

Christ came to save and heal. I can't help with the saving. I would love to save my children. Every day I think about how I wish I could save them, and I can't do it. All I can do is model for them. I can't even tell them what to do at this point. I'm grateful for the Savior, who can do that saving work.

But Christ can't do the healing part of His mission without us. We are "little s" saviors on Mount Zion. We are the ones that can interject into our relationships this spirit of selfless love and healing effort. And in that intention, the Atonement of Jesus Christ can work.

The other person in the relationship can completely reject me. They might even attack me. But as my boat leaves the harbor every day, my intention is towards love and healing. Even over the hardest things, a connection can be made and healing can happen in this selfless effort.

As I said in my book,

So this is my personal path forward. With the law of love as my guiding light, my steely foundation of faith, I can stare into the enormity of human foibles. From polygamy, racism, difficult issues in Church history, sexism, queerphobia, to anything else that can destabilize my relationship to the institutional Church, I can stare at it, chew on it, and own it. I can find the grace to manage through it without flinching. It can be devastatingly heavy and painful, but I can go back to the fundamental message of the Restoration, which is this: every single person on earth has a divine heritage from loving Heavenly Parents who knew us before; They have a plan for our growth on this earth; and Christ came to heal us and save us. . . . Every aspect of Christ's message should propel us outward to bring healing and to extend the atoning power of Christ to everyone. Every soul is rooted in faith from their very first step into mortality, and we are called to provide more space for that trajectory of faith. It's the call for each of us to rise up to Christ's message of inclusion and love.[2]

I hope the idea of Moses's two trips up the mountain makes these concepts clearer. We can grow in our ability to better see the transactional verbiage that we use with our children, spouse, siblings, or family at large, and start to catch ourselves beforehand.

In fact, my wife will many times say, "Steve, that is not the law of love." And I think, *You're right. That is not the language of the law of love, nor the spirit of the law of love*. That can happen almost daily. I got into a conflict yesterday with my daughter, and I finished that little conflict thinking that I did not use the language of the vital things that are most important in that relationship.

As we chew on this together, trying to figure it out, let's work at leaving behind transaction so that we can move forward to the higher, holier work of the law of love: loving others as God loves them, seeking their healing, expecting nothing in return. ✺

This essay was adapted from Steve Young's 2023 Restore talk.

1. *Saturday's Warrior,* a musical by Douglass Stewart and Lex de Azevedo, 1973.

2. Steve Young, *The Law of Love* (Salt Lake City: Deseret Book, 2022), 183–84.

Michael Cook

Go "visit

the

mountains

IF YE ARE PREPARED

Be Not Afraid, Only Believe

LIZZIE HEISELT

OMETIMES, FOR OUR OWN amusement, or possibly to feel like we are doing something to think about the unthinkable, my family and I imagine what we would do in the event of a catastrophe. How could we manage if the streets of our city—New York City—became unnavigable? Would we inflate our inflatable kayak, tie it to our inflatable air mattress, and paddle down the East River to the harbor and on to . . . somewhere safe? What if we needed to get out and all trains and roads were packed with other evacuees? Could we ride our bikes out of the city and halfway across the country to land with family? How could we live if we were hemmed in with few supplies? Would we be prepared to lie down together and die?

It is a morbid exercise, and yet it is never too far from our minds. Not only do world events in Ukraine, Israel, Gaza, and elsewhere have us imagining our own homes under attack or under siege, but my long-widowed mother-in-law constantly insists and encourages us to *prepare prepare prepare*. For her, that means she needs a basement full of food and supplies standing ready and waiting for the next big catastrophe. And despite our rather different circumstances— with us already packing eight people into a nine-hundred-square-foot apartment—she urges us to think creatively about how we could use our home as a storage unit as well as a living space.

She has told me she would never turn anyone away who came to her door looking for food. And suddenly to my mind spring the images of dystopian, post-apocalyptic fiction that I've seen on TV or read in novels: people scrounging for food, shooting anyone who has some, scraping by and stooping to unspeakable acts to secure their next meal. I wonder if I really want to participate in that kind of a world.

And yet, the grim task of thinking about the unthinkable—of nuclear winter, of attacks on major urban centers, of advanced climate-change disasters—seems an important mental drill, not only for our family, but for at least a substantial subset of society who make emergency preparedness and survivalism serious hobbies, or the subject of various forms of art. It is a way of playing that helps us approach those extreme possibilities and to suss out what we might need—or want—to do to survive. Perhaps this practice brings us to the realization that, ultimately, we are not in control and we must develop faith in the unknown.

But planning is something we all must do. Preparing is a way to ensure that when things

Kathryn Rees

> **What do we need to be prepared to combat or avoid? Hunger, illness, death? But we all have hungers, physical and otherwise, that may never be filled.**

go south, we will be able to rise above the fray, unafraid. We often use past experiences to help identify places in our lives that need to be shored up and protected.

When I see my mother-in-law's basement, I recognize that as a young widow, she no doubt relied heavily on her storeroom during the years when her children were young and she was not yet able to work full time. My grandmother also had a basement room with shelves stacked with canned goods. My cousins and I would make a game of finding the oldest or most bizarre food product in the place—fully cooked canned bacon from the '60s—and wonder why she didn't just throw it out. In retrospect, as a child growing up in America during the Great Depression and as a young woman during WWII, Grandma had her own memories of hunger, want, and deprivation to guard against.

I see the efforts of these strong and careful women, and I understand and applaud the wisdom of setting aside and storing up both food and money for the very real possibilities of unemployment, debilitating illness, and unexpected death. And yet, today it strikes me as both too much and not enough at the same time.

I see a mismatch in the "emergencies" of our times and the ways we have been taught to "prepare" for the unexpected. While very prudent and practical, our industrial shelving units stacked with #10 cans of dehydrated potato pearls will only get us so far in a time when loneliness, addiction, anxiety, and helplessness are emerging as the urgent issues affecting our health, our communities, and our lives.

I'm not alone in seeing a mismatch. Leaders of the Church have included sections on developing emotional resilience in the latest emergency preparedness publications. They've shifted focus from building up stores of food to helping members build greater self-reliance.

But it's not just that the "emergencies" and the "preparation" don't match, it's that focusing on the storage preparation plan can blind us to other devastating and destructive problems. When we are so focused on guarding against hunger or maintaining the maximum level of self-sufficiency, we can miss the ways in which that focus undermines our sense of community and builds a sense of false security. Beyond that, focusing on our physical preparedness that we "shall not fear"[1] is at odds with another important bit of counsel to "take therefore no thought for tomorrow"[2] and instead have faith we will be able to meet life's challenges as they arise.

So, what is it that we fear? What do we need to be prepared to combat or avoid? Hunger, illness, death? But we all have hungers, physical and otherwise, that may never be filled. We all experience illness and disease of many kinds. We all will die— some of us proverbially multiple times in multiple ways before our bodies are permanently laid to rest. And so it seems that perhaps, in addition to doing what we can to strengthen our ability to confront these physical weaknesses, we also need to live in a way that when they do become part of our experience, it is not an experience coupled with and intensified by fear.

In my mind, the counsel to be prepared must be about living in such a way that when we find ourselves in any situation, we feel that it is exactly what we have been living for, that this is just where we want to be. Like the little jar of "prepared horseradish" I keep in my fridge and sometimes mix into the filling for a supper pie or smear on a baked potato, where it adds contrast and life to the most basic of meals. The flavor and the heat also recall the many trips my family took to Arby's when I was a child, where the salty meat sandwiches were tamed and elevated by the addition of a squeeze of creamy Horsey Sauce from little plastic packets. The sauce stands by, waiting for its moment, and boldly steps in to enliven any meal. It was *prepared* for just such a thing.

In the Book of Mormon, the missionary Alma begins to look for those who need to hear the word of God. He searches in synagogues and preaches on the streets, finding that those who are most receptive are those who are "in a preparation to hear the word."[3] That is, they have been humbled by their trials, by their poverty, by the lack of dignity they have been given. They are ready to be changed from these raw, coarse, discarded people to become just the right thing that would bless, elevate, and deepen any situation they may find themselves in. They are ready to look to God, and in doing so, to truly live. Having nothing, they are ready for anything.

This is what I think of when I think, deeply and honestly, about the unknowable, unimaginable curves life can take. I think that when God said, "If ye are prepared, ye shall not fear," He was speaking less about seventy-two-hour kits and three-month supplies and more about being, as these people Alma found to teach, "in a preparation" to do or accept whatever it is the situation calls for at the moment. That is, to be humble, grounded, flexible, and open. To live our lives in such a way that when we are faced with difficulty, destruction, and even despair, we will be able to discern the best course of action step by step, led by faith.

One such example from literature is a story my elementary school librarian read to my class when I was around ten years old. Week by week, chapter by chapter, Ms. Chadwick told us the story of *Mama's Bank Account* by Kathryn Forbes, and the trials and travails of a Norwegian immigrant family trying to make their way in San Francisco in the 1920s. While the family was poor, they always had the comfort of knowing Mama had a bank account to draw upon if necessary. The family went to great lengths to protect that bank account so they would never lose the security it offered. But of course, when the children were grown and the family was more established,

Kathryn Rees

Mama revealed that she had never even been inside a bank. She had helped them through various struggles, disappointments, and missteps with a resourcefulness and faithfulness that led, in a roundabout way, to better educational opportunities, resistance to peer pressure, and a strong family culture that protected them all from the pitfalls of a life unmoored from their homeland.

Mama's family was not fearful about their survival; they were hoping to thrive in their new country, to live well. Living not merely by avoiding death, of course, but by finding joy and peace amid the chaos and confusion of daily life. Mama was well prepared, but not because she had money stored away. Her preparedness lay in her strong imagination, good will, and clear vision.

Holocaust survivor Viktor Frankl famously advocated for finding the strength within ourselves to make any situation—apocalyptic or mundane—a situation in which we can bring whatever is needed. "It [does] not really matter what we [expect] from life, but what life [expects] from us," Frankl wrote. We must "think of ourselves as being questioned by life—daily and hourly." I wonder how we prepare our answers.

How do we answer when life asks us about the "emergencies" of our day—things like anger, or loneliness, or depression? Are we prepared to reach out for help when we need it? To humbly admit when we don't have the answers? To seek out those who need the light that we carry or the rest we can provide?

It is tempting to think of our physical preparations as protection. If we didn't have a basement full of supplies, plus go-bags for every member of the family, we would surely regret it. It would be tempting fate to make fools of us. Our goods are a line of defense—but a thin and incomplete one, porous and faint. It can give us the illusion of security when in reality, it could all be taken away or rendered useless in many scenarios. It can give us the illusion of self-sufficiency and prevent us from developing the community, cooperation, and interdependence that we need most in trying times. It can weigh us down, holding us fast when what we need is freedom to move.

Can we instead develop societies that are practiced in supporting each other through the daily wear and tear of living in the world? If we can do that, we can be truly prepared for anything. We can bring peace to ourselves, our communities, our world. We can share meals with the families managing the postpartum transitions and intense cancer treatment schedules, and we can also share more moments sitting on the porch listening to children playing, watching for signs of stress, and shouldering the burdens of everyday life and earthly relationships together. Developing those connections creates a network of strength so that the inevitable internal, individual trials are not catastrophic.

Among our "emergency preparedness" supplies should be an ample amount of resilience and acceptance. We should have, in our stockpile, a practice of working through difficult emotions and finding tools to help us calm our fears so that we can think clearly to find the next right step. Our cache should include a web of strong relationships we have developed and nurtured in ways as small as a smile and nod as we pass on the street and as large as being on the front lines of support for a family facing a difficult or deadly diagnosis.

When I imagine preparing for those other scenarios, instead of inflating air mattresses and bicycle tires, I see us looking out of our windows, searching for those who may need our help. With less than nine hundred square feet to work with in our own home, I see us reaching out of our comfort and into the unknown, taking hold of it and learning about it until our discomfort abates. I scan our friends, family, neighbors, and acquaintances and recognize the gifts and strengths in each one that I could call on when my day has had a hiccup or my life has been derailed. I notice a new mom, sleep deprived and overwhelmed, and I know I can bring her a listening ear, an hour or two of rest, and the comfort of a couple of healthy meals. I recognize that I am in a preparation hoping to add whatever is needed, wherever I happen to be. ✹

1. Doctrine and Covenants 38:30.

2. Matthew 6:34.

3. Alma 32:6.

can a

womb   forget

her

shame

?

ON BRUCE R. McCONKIE

JOSEPH
SPENCER

Much of what we think about
Bruce R. McConkie today is wrong.

IN 2005, THE UNIVERSITY OF UTAH
Press issued *David O. McKay and the Rise of Modern Mormonism*, written by Gregory Prince and Robert Wright. It is a crucial contribution to the study of Latter-day Saint history. But I find it striking that, over the nearly two decades of the book's circulation, I've seen and heard one anecdote from it cited far more often than any other. It's about Bruce R. McConkie and what Prince and Wright call "the controversy over *Mormon Doctrine*."[1]

Today, the anecdote is perhaps so well known that it doesn't need repeating, but here's a refresher, taken straight from the biography:

> [President] McKay's initial reaction to [Mormon Doctrine, originally published in 1958] was not favorable. He summoned two senior apostles, Mark E. Petersen and Marion G. Romney [and] asked them if they would together go over Elder Bruce R. McConkie's book. Petersen and Romney took ten months to critique the book and make their report to the First Presidency. Romney submitted a lengthy letter on January 7, 1960, [and] Petersen gave McKay an oral report in which he recommended 1,067 corrections that "affected most of the 776 pages of the book." The following day, McKay and his counselors made their decision. The book "must not be republished, as it is full of errors and misstatements."[2]

As interesting as this story is in its own right, I find myself far more interested in why Latter-day Saint intellectuals have been so taken by it.

There is, of course, the obvious reason. The sheer influence of *Mormon Doctrine* within The Church of Jesus Christ of Latter-day Saints from the time of its publication to the end of the twentieth century can hardly be overstated. It was so often treated among the Saints as the final court of appeals on what constitutes the official doctrine of the Church (consider its ubiquity in the form of quotations throughout Church-published materials until the early 2000s) that the story of its rocky beginnings naturally registered to many as a marvel. And because so many academically inclined Latter-day Saints had their own doubts and suspicions about many claims made and many conclusions drawn in *Mormon Doctrine*, they could welcome news that the President of the Church at the time of its publication was, effectively, on their side.

Vindication, in a word. Hopefully without a spirit of vindictiveness.

But vindication, I think, isn't enough of an explanation. The fact is that Bruce R. McConkie and *Mormon Doctrine* have been treated unfairly, in many regards. There's more to what both the man and his work represented for the historical development of the Latter-day Saint faith than is generally allowed. This is not to say that anyone should feel bound to agree with any particular claims or conclusions in a book like *Mormon Doctrine*. It's certainly not to excuse certain deeply problematic things said in that work or elsewhere (about race especially). It's rather to say that there's too much of the boogeyman in the common portrait that Latter-day Saint intellectuals paint of McConkie.

It's time for a reassessment. And that means that it's time for a little context.

In 1965, the University of Utah Press issued philosopher Sterling McMurrin's book *The*

Photo-illustration of Bruce R. McConkie by Esther H. Candari

Theological Foundations of the Mormon Religion. It remains important despite its age, at the very least because there exist so few scholarly attempts to draw together the whole of Latter-day Saint thought. But probably more important for the lasting significance of McMurrin's book is the timing of its original publication. The appearance of *Theological Foundations* was exactly contemporary with the formal organization of the Mormon History Association, with the towering historian Leonard Arrington as its first president. Arrington's leadership of what would soon be called "the New Mormon History" would prove to be of immense and lasting cultural importance.

In 1965, it seems, the question was whether theology or history marked the way forward for Latter-day Saint intellectuals. And as of 1965, the question was still undecided. Arrington and McMurrin, the historian and the philosopher, were contemporaries with a similar sense of the obstacle that then faced Latter-day Saint intellectual culture. They nonetheless had almost entirely opposite ideas about how to tackle that obstacle.

McMurrin made clear at the end of *Theological Foundations* what he took to be the obstacle for Latter-day Saint intellectuals. He concluded the volume with a few reflections "on the task of Mormon theology."[3] "Yesterday," he wrote, Latter-day Saint theology "was vigorous, prophetic, and creative; today it is timid and academic and prefers scholastic rationalization to the adventure of ideas."[4] What had crept into Latter-day Saint intellectual culture? McMurrin pointed above all to "the impact of religious and social conservatism" and to "the seductions of irrationalism."[5] As *Theological Foundations* and other writings by McMurrin make perfectly clear,[6] he worried that the Saints had followed in their own way a larger Christian trend in the mid-twentieth century—that of neo-orthodoxy.[7] That is, representatives of the tradition were talking more of divine grace and less of human potential, emphasizing the limits of human rationality and declaring that divine revelation is transparent and incontestable. McMurrin found all this philosophically and theologically disappointing.

It's perfectly clear whose passing McMurrin lamented: James E. Talmage, John A. Widtsoe, and

Photo-illustration of Hugh Nibley by Esther H. Candari

especially B. H. Roberts—the great Progressive Era thinkers who outlined the possibility that Joseph Smith's teachings embodied an optimistic humanism. It's also perfectly clear whose rise McMurrin found discouraging. There were two figures who represented the new Latter-day Saint theology. First, there was the erudite historian of antiquity whom McMurrin regarded as "the strangest aberration that has ever afflicted Mormonism": Hugh Nibley.[8] In McMurrin's view, though, Nibley wasn't a theologian; he was a historian. But, in McMurrin's view, Nibley did little more than labor to arrange historical data to bolster the new theology. Nibley, in short, wasn't the architect of the new theology but a builder of walls around it.

Who, then, was hard at work within the walls of that new theology itself? Without a doubt, for McMurrin, it was Bruce R. McConkie. It was McConkie's thought that he regarded as "timid and academic," preferring "scholastic rationalization to the adventure of ideas." Nibley enjoyed the life of the mind, but McMurrin believed he was putting all of his best intellectual efforts in the service of defending a theological vision that was antagonistic toward the life of the mind.

The case can be made that it was the same cultural development—the rise of Bruce R. McConkie—that motivated the New Mormon History led by Leonard Arrington. Especially telling is what Jan Shipps once said was "the mantra of the LDS intellectual community" during the formative years of the New Mormon History: "Mormonism does not have a theology; it has a history."[9] The idea, it seems, was that doctrinal elaboration and theological systematizing rightly found their places in other forms of Christianity. Latter-day Saints, the historians claimed, sacralized its past rather than any system of thought—such that, if there was something that might be called a Latter-day Saint theology, it simply was the Church's history. At any rate, it was apparently clear to someone coming from the outside (Shipps was not a Latter-day Saint) that the historical project was in large part driven by a felt need to *stop* the flow of Latter-day Saint theology. It was perhaps viewed as commendable that there *had* been robust Latter-day Saint theological activity in the past, but it was apparently felt that such previous work should be treated as an archive for historical reflection rather than a resource for further theological speculation.

Why such antipathy in the mid-1960s toward the very idea that the Saints might "have a theology"? The most obvious answer by far is simply that Bruce R. McConkie's writings left Latter-day Saint intellectuals with little hope for the theological enterprise as such. Given Elder McConkie's strongly authoritarian streak, it was safer by far for scholars to settle their minds in intellectual territories where his flag wasn't flying. Moreover, historians might well have reasoned, if one could slowly convince others (and even the institutional Church!) that "Mormonism does not have a theology; it has a history," then the influence of a book like *Mormon Doctrine* could be trusted to fade in time. In the meantime, intellectually inclined Latter-day Saints had plenty of room to do interesting work without doing theology.

In retrospect, then, McMurrin and Arrington might be viewed as having seen the challenge to

> **Because so many academically inclined Latter-day Saints had their own doubts and suspicions about many claims made and many conclusions drawn in *Mormon Doctrine*, they could welcome news that the President of the Church at the time of its publication was, effectively, on their side.**

Latter-day Saint intellectual life in 1965 in similar ways. They developed strikingly different strategies for moving forward, however. The historians, in essence, wagered that the passing of the early twentieth-century theological vision was lamentable but irreversible, and so the task for Latter-day Saint intellectuals was now to historicize what had passed. McMurrin, by contrast, wagered that there might be enough life in the Latter-day Saint intellectual community to revive the passing theological project and so to mobilize it against what he saw rising. Either way, it seems, both parties believed that what was needed above all was an alternative to Bruce R. McConkie.

Who was Bruce R. McConkie? It's perhaps worth providing just a sketch of this towering figure, especially because collective memory of him has begun to fade.[10]

Eventually, McConkie came to be known as an astonishingly bright but unmistakably authoritarian Latter-day Saint leader. He began, though, as an aspiring young professional (in law and business). But just into his adulthood, he married the daughter of then-Apostle (and later Church President) Joseph Fielding Smith (who in turn was the grandnephew of founding prophet Joseph Smith). Following his father-in-law's intellectual footsteps while he pursued his professional training, the young man soaked up writings by American Evangelicals and other conservative Christians who contended against modernizing trends and developed an intense interest in doctrine. He himself would eventually define doctrine as "the tenets, teachings, and true theories found in the scriptures; . . . the principles, precepts, and revealed philosophies of pure religion; [and] prophetic dogmas, maxims, and views."[11] Its exposition and systematization became his life's passion.

Bruce McConkie became Elder McConkie in 1946, moving into general Church leadership (as what is now called a President of the Seventy) in his early thirties. Beyond his ecclesiastical duties, he gave the decade of the 1950s to compiling Fielding Smith's teachings into a three-volume compendium, as well as penning his own influential theological encyclopedia of sorts, the already-mentioned monolithic *Mormon Doctrine*, which appeared in 1958.[12] He then spent the 1960s writing a three-volume doctrinal commentary on the New Testament, the last volume of which appeared in 1972—the year he became an Apostle. Elder McConkie gave his final years (he died in 1985) to writing doctrinal treatises on Latter-day Saint Christology, as well as what he called *A New Witness for the Articles of Faith*.[13] His final public testimony, offered in general conference shortly before his death, has often been praised as a classic of Latter-day Saint devotional oratory.[14]

It's hard to overstate Elder McConkie's influence on Latter-day Saint culture and thought in the second half of the twentieth century—despite the labors of the New Mormon History to create an intellectual alternative to his thinking. This is especially true because he absorbed into himself the already enormous cultural and intellectual authority of his father-in-law (first and most influentially by serving as editor for the three-volume collection of his father-in-law's teachings). A lawyer by training but a theologian by disposition, McConkie wedded the rigor of courtroom

Photo-illustration of Sterling McMurrin by Esther H. Candari

argumentation to a commonsense approach to the meaning of Latter-day Saint scripture. The result was a layman's rationalism: profound trust in the capacities of the mind, so long as that mind was bridled by unswerving loyalty to the Church. Beginning with *Mormon Doctrine*, McConkie essentially labored at producing a Latter-day Saint theological system that naturally appealed to conservatively minded believers who nonetheless had strong intellectual inclinations.

What this meant, above all, was that his writings came like manna from heaven to teachers in (what was then called) the Division of Religion at Brigham Young University and in the Church's seminaries and institutes of religion. In search of something more than manuals to satisfy their curious minds but unsure about the boundless expanse of academic research, they found in McConkie what they most wished for. For decades, the vast majority of the Church's active younger members, especially in the United States, went through these programs and so were shaped by a heavy dose of McConkie-inspired instruction. Thus, by the 1970s and continuing to the end of the 1990s, whatever McConkie called "Mormon doctrine" basically *was* Mormon doctrine, its

dissemination subsidized by the Church (eventually in a formal manner: quoted liberally throughout Church publications).

In 1965, though, McConkie's project was still young. His first book, *Mormon Doctrine*, was only seven years old, and his second (the first volume of the *Doctrinal New Testament Commentary*) appeared just that year. McConkie wouldn't become an Apostle until seven years later. It was clear that what McConkie was spearheading would end up having real cultural force, but its fortunes weren't entirely clear yet. All that was apparently clear to both the historians working under Arrington and the lone-voice philosopher McMurrin was that something else needed to be on offer.

The year 1965 now sounds like a long time ago. What has happened since?

There's a relatively standard way of recounting the years since 1965. McMurrin ended up busy with other things, despite his plea for new work

in Latter-day Saint theology. Here and there a work of theology in a style more recognizably academic than McConkie's would appear, but these were unrepresentative of the "vigorous" thinking McMurrin saw himself as calling for.[15] Theology disappeared or went underground for a time.[16] Meanwhile, the historians went on to striking success, their influence waxing in the 1960s and '70s, waning in the turbulent 1980s and early '90s (when, curiously, certain theological debates plagued the historical conversation), but then exploding in the new millennium.[17] Only when historical work broadened into the discipline of Mormon studies early in the twenty-first century did it begin to appear that there might be space again for theology's possibilities as McMurrin once envisioned them. Works on Latter-day Saint theology suddenly began to appear, and then to proliferate, and the theologically inclined began to professionalize.

Theology, it would seem, was rather suddenly back after a long hiatus. It took nearly half a century, but McMurrin's call could finally be answered afresh in the early twenty-first century—if for no other reason than that the influence of Bruce R. McConkie began to fade

Photo-illustration of Bruce R. McConkie by Esther H. Candari

after the eventual successes of the historians. And the new wave of Latter-day Saint theologians swelling in the first decade of the twenty-first century—led, in so many ways, by Blake Ostler[18]—often laid claim to the same early twentieth-century thinkers that McMurrin had summarized and celebrated in his 1965 book: Talmage, Widtsoe, and Roberts. Had McMurrin lived just a little longer, he might have been cheered to see his vision realized at last.

This, as I say, is the usual way of telling the story of the past six decades. And it may be that this way of telling the story will prevail. After all, Latter-day Saints are familiar with stories of falling away and restoration, so perhaps such a telling feels natural. But there's a subset of Latter-day Saint theologians working in the first quarter of the twenty-first century that, I think, this story doesn't account for. Thinkers of this other sort include James Faulconer, Rosalynde Welch, Adam Miller, Kimberly Matheson, and others. (I count myself among them.) Such thinkers have apparently found McMurrin's account of Latter-day Saint theology largely unhelpful, have mostly ignored Talmage and Widtsoe and Roberts, have been somewhat puzzled by the intellectual styles of many contemporary Latter-day Saint thinkers (despite having deep respect for them), and have wondered why so little work in contemporary Latter-day Saint theology focuses on the concrete realities of lived faith. Perhaps above all, such thinkers have wondered about the at-best *occasional* role played by scripture in so much of Latter-day Saint thought today. These other theologians' points of orientation have lain elsewhere, and their methods of proceeding have been otherwise, than those of their contemporaries.

Where did they—or, really, we—come from? I shouldn't speak for others, but I will venture a hypothesis. *We other theologians are the continuation—albeit with certain obvious reservations—of the intellectual project launched by Bruce R. McConkie.* We were, I wager, shaped intellectually and devotionally far more by the concerns and interests of the Church Educational System than by any strong sense of resistance to it. To be sure, we share few of McConkie's particular conclusions, but we *do* share something like the

A lawyer by training but a theologian by disposition, McConkie wedded the rigor of courtroom argumentation to a commonsense approach to the meaning of Latter-day Saint scripture. The result was a layman's rationalism: profound trust in the capacities of the mind, so long as that mind was bridled by unswerving loyalty to the Church.

same animating spirit. Yes, our methods have been shaped by our own professional training (generally in and around the so-called "continental" style of philosophy) rather than by the legal profession, but we tend to think that McConkie was right to bring all the rigor he could to the life of faith. An especially important difference is that McConkie consistently claimed to speak *for* the Church, while we only offer our work to the Church in the hopes that it's useful—but this means that we, like McConkie, see our thinking as being in the service of the Restoration more than of the academy.

And, above all, there's scripture. It has far too seldom been noted that McConkie, whatever else one wishes to say about him, more or less single-handedly convinced two or three generations of Latter-day Saints that their faith had to be worked out through an unswervingly dedicated study of the unique set of scriptural books embraced by the Saints. Remember that he wrote a three-volume doctrinal—that is, theological—commentary on the New Testament. That a Latter-day Saint thinker ventured to do such a thing more than fifty years ago boggles the mind, really. Something like McConkie's conviction regarding the import of scripture has, above all, guided our—or, at the very least, *my*—work as a theologian.

Why make scripture a hard foundation for the future of Latter-day Saint thought? Should Latter-day Saint thinkers feel so beholden to texts that come from increasingly distant historical periods, increasingly foreign worlds? For my money, yes, and for a host of reasons. I'll name just three for the moment.

First, Latter-day Saint scripture is almost certain to have more sticking power than anything else current today within the Latter-day Saint context. Whatever the future of this particular religious tradition looks like, there's almost certain to be periodic returns to, say, the Book of Mormon. Second, scripture is something that sits in the hands of every member of the Church, such that reflection beginning from these texts is most likely to matter to those trying to work out their relationship to God. If theology is to make a difference to anyone beyond the walls of the academy, scripture is likely to be the vehicle that carries it there. Third, scripture, if it's read carefully and consistently, refuses to allow the academically inclined to reduce it to mere systems of abstract concepts. Scripture is messy and complicated, its increasing historical distance illustrative of such complexity—and honesty in reading it can only help prevent the theological endeavor from flattening faith into something foreign to real life.

Are there challenges? No doubt. The study of Latter-day Saint scripture is still young. What scholarship exists that might be useful to theological readers has been driven not only by historical but by historicist tendencies, resulting in too many ventures that have been overly sure of their hypotheses and given to reductionist interpretations as a result.[19] Further, many texts in the canon leave readers with troubling ethical concerns that need addressing in responsible ways. Further still, very little academic support exists at present to harbor the serious study of Latter-day Saint scripture—whether for theological purposes or otherwise—and so the incentives are few for drawing real expertise to the task of interpretation. There are, in short, any number of hurdles to clear. It's worth the effort to clear them, however, to give Latter-day Saint theology a center of gravity, so that it's far less prone to be "carried about with every wind of doctrine" (Ephesians 4:14).

Not long after the historians took the stage in the 1960s, they began to speak of a "lost generation" of historians—historians like Juanita Brooks and Dale Morgan who wrote in the 1930s and '40s and made major contributions that, because they were ahead of their time, too easily went unnoticed. I think it's time to recognize another lost generation, a lost generation of theologians. Bruce R. McConkie deserves reinvestigation. Latter-day Saint scholars haven't yet asked why he did what he did, how he went about it, and with what intellectual effects. It's time to do so. What did he—and those who worked in his wake for two or three decades—contribute to Latter-day Saint thought, and in what ways does today's theological work build on foundations laid by such surprising forebears?

Latter-day Saints have, from almost the very beginning, taken the redemption of their ancestors to be among their divinely appointed responsibilities. We scour census records, visit parish archives, learn how to use microfilm, and rifle through attic treasure chests—all in the hope of recovering the lives and the legacies of those who would otherwise fade from our collective memory. Shouldn't we feel as bound to the thinkers and theologians of our own faith tradition's past as we do to the similarly flawed but lovable people who have forged our individual families' histories? Theological reading of scripture comes to the present out of the past, and sometimes from uncomfortable quarters. But Bruce R. McConkie shouldn't be mummified and sealed away in a crypt, left for historians of the distant future to speculate about. We have something to learn from him right now—or something that we've already learned from him that's alive right now.

The shape of future Latter-day Saint thought may depend on how honest we are about, and how faithful we are to, our theological past. ✳

Photo-illustration of Sterling McMurrin by Esther H. Candari

1. Gregory A. Prince and Wm. Robert Wright, *David O. McKay and the Rise of Modern Mormonism* (Salt Lake City: University of Utah Press, 2005), 49.

2. Prince and Wright, *David O. McKay*, 50–51. For simplicity's sake, I have eliminated ellipses in this quotation, condensing into a shorter report what Prince and Wright recount in more detail. Note that all quotations within this quotation come from David O. McKay's personal diary.

3. Sterling M. McMurrin, *The Theological Foundation of the Mormon Religion* (Salt Lake City: University of Utah Press, 1965), 110.

4. McMurrin, *Theological Foundation*, 112.

5. McMurrin, *Theological Foundation*, 111.

6. See McMurrin, *Theological Foundation*; and also throughout Sterling M. McMurrin, *Religion, Reason, and Truth: Historical Essays in the Philosophy of Religion* (Salt Lake City: University of Utah Press, 1982).

7. For a fuller elaboration of McMurrin's view, albeit in the voice of a disciple, see O. Kendall White Jr., *Mormon Neo-Orthodoxy: A Crisis Theology* (Salt Lake City: Signature Books, 1987).

8. Letter by Sterling McMurrin to Hugh Nibley, dated November 1, 1960, Hugh Nibley Papers, box 40, L. Tom Perry Special Collections, Brigham Young University.

9. Jan Shipps, *Sojourner in the Promised Land: Forty Years among the Mormons* (Urbana and Chicago: University of Illinois Press, 2000), 381.

10. The only full biography of Bruce R. McConkie is Joseph Fielding McConkie, *The Bruce R. McConkie Story: Reflections of a Son* (Salt Lake City: Deseret Book, 2003).

11. Bruce R. McConkie, *Mormon Doctrine*, 2nd ed. (Salt Lake City: Bookcraft, 1966), 204.

12. See Joseph Fielding Smith, *Doctrines of Salvation*, 3 vols., ed. Bruce R. McConkie (Salt Lake City: Deseret Book, 1954–56); and Bruce R. McConkie, *Mormon Doctrine*, 1st ed. (Salt Lake City: Bookcraft, 1958).

13. See Bruce R. McConkie, *Doctrinal New Testament Commentary*, 3 vols. (Salt Lake City: Bookcraft, 1965–72); Bruce R. McConkie, *The Messiah Series*, 6 vols. (Salt Lake City: Deseret Book, 1978–82); and Bruce R. McConkie, *A New Witness for the Articles of Faith* (Salt Lake City: Deseret Book, 1985).

14. Text and video can be found at Bruce R. McConkie, "The Purifying Power of Gethsemane," *Ensign*, May 1985, 9–11, churchofjesuschrist.org.

15. The most celebrated work of Latter-day Saint theology in the later twentieth century is arguably Truman G. Madsen, *Eternal Man* (Salt Lake City: Deseret Book, 1966). As James Faulconer says of this book, it "was not academically profound, but then it had no pretensions to be." For Faulconer, its primary impact was in its suggestion to aspiring Latter-day Saint intellectuals that there was "room to talk" about theology. James E. Faulconer, *Faith, Philosophy, Scripture* (Provo, UT: Neal A. Maxwell Institute, 2010), 19.

16. It helped that Hugh Nibley was publicly making the case that theology was what sent Christianity off the rails in the fourth century, necessitating the much-later Restoration through Joseph Smith and the Book of Mormon. See especially Hugh Nibley, *The World and the Prophets* (Salt Lake City: Deseret Book, 1954).

17. The history is recounted ably in Ronald W. Walker, David J. Whittaker, and James B. Allen, *Mormon History* (Urbana and Chicago: University of Illinois Press, 2010).

18. Not only do the four volumes of Ostler's *Explorations in Mormon Thought* carry out a program not dissimilar to McMurrin's in certain (but not all!) regards, Ostler arguably made his first marks in the Latter-day Saint intellectual community when he published a long and important interview with McMurrin. See Blake Ostler and Sterling M. McMurrin, "An Interview with Sterling McMurrin," *Dialogue: A Journal of Mormon Thought* 17, no. 1 (Fall–Winter 1983): 18–43.

19. I have commented on this business of historicism elsewhere. See throughout Joseph M. Spencer, *The Anatomy of Book of Mormon Theology*, 2 vols. (Salt Lake City: Greg Kofford Books, 2021).

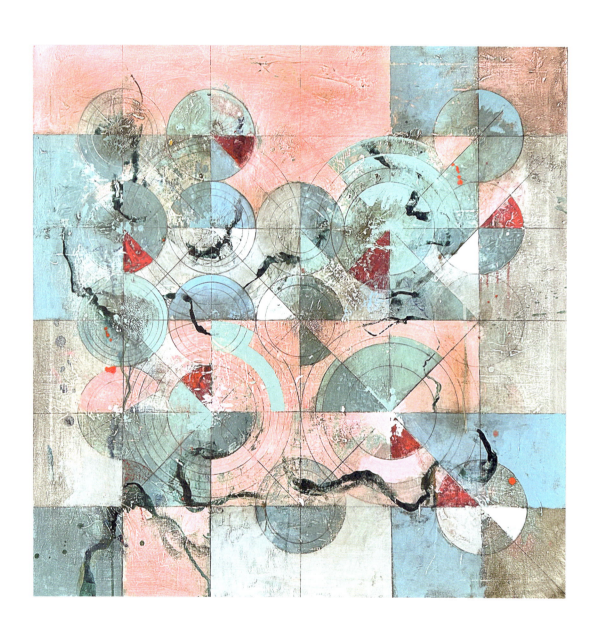

Nathan Mulford

ANNUNCIATION

LAURA
REECE
HOGAN

This is your tender demand: *look to me.*
My eyes bore into the hairline cracks
zigzagging the table. You lift my gaze up
and across and out

the room to an illumination I didn't expect.
I'd bought that painting so many years ago,
Mary draped in violet and sapphire opposite
the red urgency of Gabriel—they had rushed

my heart, so vibrant on some kind
of stretched translucent canvas, almost like skin,
almost like pain. Not quite an icon, with broken
planes and imperfections, electric angel striding

in the viewer's space, intent on delivering the earth-
quake. Mary's face ashen, brows drawn, gazing
at not the angel, not the fractured fretwork of floor,
but at someone beyond, her still, slim fingers looped

in forgotten crimson threads. From the room
a room away I saw the scene as I'd never seen it, all
those years: the first morning gleams kindling
silvered oils, quickening the luster of a bow

plunging into the two fraught figures,
the light dynamic, velvet with something almost
like peace. *From this perspective,* you say.
I won't let you miss.

WORK OF THE UNKNOWN PETITIONER

LAURA
REECE
HOGAN

Where my words burrow soft
I do not know, yet watch the sky fold velvet,

tend to the blue,
spatter liberation to the drought-stricken

fields. You know me, though you've never
witnessed me. I blow the whiskery globe

of dandelion, it's my prayer
hinging the light, just beyond the corner of your

nightstand, of your drainpipe,
my prayer a thing so prosaic, immaterial—yet

see the heart wrecked, hard
intractable crust over a hidden sea of tenderness,

gold at the core—let me enter, unknown. Let me
be the sigh, the shelter, unobserved.

Let this slender nothing, these wisps floating upward
hammer and hew a home.

Kristin Carver

ANXIOUSLY ENGAGED

In Weakness, Strength

STAN BENFELL

'M TRYING TO REMEMBER THE moment when I realized that I am an anxious man. When I was growing up in the 1970s and as a young adult in the 1980s, we never talked about "anxiety" as a mental health issue, and so I assumed that my way of experiencing the world was not unusual. The moment of realization may have been the first time one of my children, all of whom have inherited my anxiety to some degree, began to demonstrate anxiousness. Or it may have been when I was sitting in elders quorum and received a new home teaching assignment to help someone I did not know. Or perhaps it was shortly after I finished my PhD and started attending academic conferences. While my best friend from graduate school moved through these conferences with ease, I struggled to feel comfortable. When we attended a conference reception, he was quickly involved in a conversation or two, while I hovered at the edges. In fact, if I met someone at a conference, it was usually because he introduced me.

I have trouble pinpointing my moment of realization, because although when I reflect back, I can see that I have been anxious for as long as I can recall, for many decades I was not aware that I was "anxious." I simply assumed that others felt the same way about meeting new people or confronting a difficult social situation but that they masked it, as I usually tried to do. Only gradually, and with increased awareness of anxiety as a mental health issue, did I realize that I was in fact suffering from anxiety, that I am an anxious individual, and that my way of seeing the world is not as common as I had assumed.

When I am asked to describe what my anxiety feels like, I usually say that it is a lot like fear. The two feelings, in fact, are so similar that I am tempted to say that anxiety makes me a coward. There's a good deal of truth in that statement, although it is nothing like the whole truth. At certain moments in my life, for example, I have done something awkward or foolish, have felt embarrassed and ashamed, and so have realized my worst social fears. But that's only the beginning of the experience, as the shame and embarrassment persist; I relive my actions, as well as the moments leading up to them, wishing that I could go back and make a different choice, or perhaps avoid the situation altogether. For a time, it seems like I live in shame, breathe it every minute of the day, and the only thing that I am able to think and resolve is: I will never feel this way again, not if I can help it.

Indeed, I have learned that whenever I contemplate a new and therefore anxiety-inducing situation, my mind immediately assumes the worst possible outcome—an outcome, when seen from any rational perspective, that has a minuscule chance of actually occurring, but one that in the moment of anticipation seems all too likely. To return to the academic conference, if I meet a scholar whose work I have read and admired, I imagine that she will scorn my work, and that I will compound things by making a social mistake, and as a result she will spread her dismal opinion of me throughout our small scholarly community. Of course, things never proceed according to my worst imaginings, but that does not stop me from assuming the worst the next time I am confronted with a new social situation. And so, my "fight or flight" response invariably defaults to flight.

And in addition to cowardice, the frequent practical effect of my anxiety is narcissism. It's so hard to get out of my own head that I have difficulty thinking about anyone else. As my daughter put her experience with anxiety to me one day, "my brain is so loud." A couple of years ago, I struggled with an inability to talk to a young man in my ward who had strayed in a public way but who was nevertheless brave enough to come back to church. As I thought of approaching him, I ran through various scenarios in my mind, most of which involved putting my foot in my mouth and perhaps in some strange way indicating that I approved of the particular way he had strayed. And so I stayed away—ashamed but caught in a web of my own conflicting thoughts. I was describing this situation to my therapist, and he illustrated it by drawing stick figures of people facing each other in conversation; he then drew thought balloons over their heads, not to indicate words or thoughts, but instead to represent their focus of attention. Most people, or at least loving people, direct virtually all of their attention to the person standing in front of them and so have only one "focus balloon" over their heads. They don't get lost for words because they are engaged with the person in front of them, seeing what that person needs. I, however, have two focus balloons. The one in front, the one directed toward the person in front of me, is small, since it represents only about 10 percent of my

James Rees

attention. The one that represents the other 90 percent is directed inwards, back onto my own mind, as I keep fretting and turning over possible scenarios and words in my head but not actually saying anything. It is no wonder that I find no words to speak, because I'm not actually thinking about the person in front of me but about my own worry, my own fear of doing something awkward or embarrassing. And so all too often this worry leads me to hang back.

There is a passage in Bruce Hafen's biography of Neal A. Maxwell that resonates with me in a surprising way. It's early in the biography, but it recounts an event late in Elder Maxwell's life. He has been diagnosed with leukemia and is about to check into the hospital to undergo a brutal series of treatments that are not much better than the cancer itself. As they park, Neal takes his wife Colleen's hand and says, "I just don't want to *shrink*."[1] I share Elder Maxwell's worry; I too don't want to shrink, although I am not facing anything as daunting as the leukemia treatment awaiting Elder Maxwell. And yet my natural response often *is* to shrink, to slink away when confronted with a challenging situation, assuming that I will not be able to handle it and will end up embarrassing myself and making the situation worse. I need to actively fight my natural desire to shrink.

And yet the idea that anxiety makes me a coward and a narcissist is also false, utterly false. Because I do not believe, in my case in any event, that my anxiety is such that it overwhelms me to the point that I no longer have a choice. I will at times let myself off the hook for failing in a social or ministering situation, but I don't think God ever does. By that I don't mean that my failure is unforgivable, but simply that He always wants me to do more and be better. Anxiety, to put it another way, is simply the condition of my life, and I have learned that there are ways to deal with it.

Several years ago, I was in London on a research leave to work at the British Library. I had a regular practice of a morning walk to Holland Park—one of my favorite places in London. At least half of the park is wooded, and for a brief time you can feel like you're not in the city. On the edge of this wooded section is the Kyoto Garden, a beautiful and serene space constructed by a Japanese landscape designer as a gift from the city of Kyoto in honor of the friendship between Japan and Great Britain. Without fail, I ended up in this garden, and when I found myself alone I would often sit for a while and pray. With some exceptions, I am not very adept at prayer. My mind is too loud, it wanders too incessantly, and I find that I have a hard time making a connection with God, since my thoughts all too often bend back to myself. But occasionally, sitting in that beautiful place, out of doors, I was able to direct my attention away from myself enough to engage in meaningful prayer. I remember one morning in particular when I expressed frustration with my anxiety and with my seeming inability to improve, wondering why my anxiety always seemed to get in the way of any serious progress. Why wouldn't the Lord simply lift my anxiety from me? As I spoke my complaint, the thought came to me unmistakably—your anxiety is your cross, your thorn in the flesh, and you will have to carry it as best you can.

And as I have tried to lift this cross through my sixty years of life, I have found that the best way to carry it is to be an active member of The Church of Jesus Christ of Latter-day Saints, to be engaged as fully as I can, even if that engagement is almost always fraught with anxiety. At first, this may well strike readers as strange. As I have visited with other anxious people who are active in the Church, I hear concerns and even complaints that resonate with my experience. What about the charge to get out of your comfort zone? Well, what if your comfort zone is not all that comfortable? What if going to church and doing what you already do makes you uncomfortable? Doesn't being engaged in the Church exacerbate anxiety? All I can say is that in my experience, the answer is no.

Part of this is due to the unexpected fact that my anxiety lessens as I occupy a particular and

And yet the idea that anxiety makes me a coward and a narcissist is also false, utterly false.

defined role. For example, if I were asked to name an activity that would create the most anxiety for me, it might well be going door-to-door and talking to people I don't know about something that they don't want to hear. This most anxious of activities, however, describes the vast majority of my days in the France Paris Mission. And yet, once I shifted into that missionary role, I was able to knock on doors, talk to people on the street or on the train, and not be debilitated by anxiety, as I felt that I was acting as a missionary was supposed to act. Similarly, when I was called as the bishop of my home ward, I found it easier to approach a member's home and knock on the door with no prior notice, because, after all, that's what bishops do.

I have already described how much of my life has an undercurrent of fear, and how often my initial response is to do whatever it takes to get out of an anxious situation, and yet being called as bishop (or a missionary) is to be thrust into countless anxious situations. Indeed, wouldn't my default flight response help me here, simply by allowing me to say no to the calling? When the stake executive secretary called me on a Saturday morning many years ago, asking my wife and me

> I recognize that when I have not followed my instinct to flee but have instead moved forward, trying my best not to resist Jesus's command but to trust in his promise that his burden is easy, I have been most fully and effectively engaged in the life of faith.

to meet with the stake president the following day, I knew what he was going to ask me to do, and I spent a rough night, sleeping little as I wrestled with the calling I knew was coming and wondered if I could say no to it.

In addition, the bishop who preceded me was Matt Holland (now Elder Holland of the Seventy), and he was a remarkable bishop. I had a close view of his talents and devotion as I served as his first counselor. When I learned that he would be moving out of the ward and so would need to be released, I remember thinking that I pitied the man who would be called to follow him. And yet here I was. As I was getting dressed on that Sunday morning, I had a strong spiritual impression that this calling came from the Lord, and that I should accept it; flight was not an option. When I met with the stake president later that morning, and he extended the call, he advised me not to try to be like Bishop Holland but to find my own way. "Ah," I remember thinking, "that advice will be easy to follow," since I had no illusions about my ability to imitate Matt. But I also knew that for members of the ward, Matt's release and my call would be a disappointment, and another cause for my anxiety.

And so when I accepted the call, I realized that I would need to remember that spiritual impression I had on that Sunday morning: for some reason, the Lord, knowing my anxiety as well as everything else about me, had called me, and I

needed to trust in that understanding. I therefore made a determination that while I was bishop, I was not going to let my anxiety rule my life. I fulfilled that determination fitfully and imperfectly, but for periods of time, I found myself, I won't say comfortable in the role of bishop, but able to fulfill the calling with some effectiveness. One of the things that I learned to appreciate in being a bishop was that the "flight" response was ruled out, and not only when I was first called. Throughout the time of my call I needed to sit down and listen to people while they talked through the challenges and heartbreaks of their lives and to have faith that I could help. Still, after every Sunday afternoon and Wednesday evening of interviews, as I drove home from the bishop's office I would pray that my anxiety and other shortcomings would not adversely influence those I had counseled.

There were even times that my anxiousness helped me in my calling, as my lack of confidence in knowing how to help people or what to say made me rely more fully on the Lord than I had at any other time in my life. When baffling situations confronted me, if I would remember the impression that the Lord had called me and wanted me in that particular position at that moment of time, I would ask for help, and an answer would come. I remember a few instances when I was counseling with an individual over a difficult situation or question, and in my flippant way prayed silently, "You've got to help me here, because I got nothing." And then suddenly, I found myself saying something that helped or that provided an answer to the question we were considering.

There is a passage in Dietrich Bonhoeffer's book *The Cost of Discipleship* in which he seeks to lay out the difficulty and cost of being a follower of Christ and of avoiding what he calls "cheap grace," the "grace" that demands nothing of the would-be disciple—no transformation and no repentance. And so he delineates all that Jesus asks of those who seek to be his disciples. As he points out, the demand is heavy, often extreme. But what, then, are we to make of Jesus's saying, "my yoke is easy, and my burden is light" (Matthew 11:30)? Bonhoeffer's answer is that only when disciples "unremittingly let his yoke rest upon" them does the burden become easy, "and under its gentle pressure [the would-be disciple] receives the power to persevere in the right way. The command of Jesus is hard, unutterably hard, for those who try to resist it. But for those who willingly submit, the yoke is easy, and the burden is light."[2] I feel the truth of Bonhoeffer's reading, but I find it very hard to "willingly submit." At times, it is excruciatingly difficult, since my natural instinct to hold back and shrink works against the demand simply to submit to what the Lord asks. But as I look back on my life, I recognize that when I have not followed my instinct to flee but have instead moved forward, trying my best not to resist Jesus's command but to trust in his promise that his burden is easy, I have been most fully and effectively engaged in the life of faith—in the Church, in my job, and in my family—and somehow that life of faith has been easier than my usual practice of avoidance.

It has now been several years since my release as bishop, and ever since I have been seeking to exercise faith in the absence of such a demanding calling. We have, after all, agreed at baptism to represent Christ *always*, to "stand as witnesses of God at all times and in all things, and in all places that [we] may be in" (Mosiah 18:9). In retrospect, demanding callings helped me to channel my anxiety productively, as I did not need to make daily decisions about moving forward, even when it meant putting myself in anxiety-inducing positions; it felt like those decisions had already been made, and I had to sink or swim. As I leaned into the tasks of the calling, trusting in its inspiration, I found that more often than not I swam. I still felt anxious while doing so, but by acting in faith my anxiety became more manageable.

I have thought a lot about the verse in Ether 12:27, where the Lord tells Moroni that he will make our weakness become strong if we exercise faith. The Lord has indeed at times made my weakness of anxiety strong, but that has not meant—even in those moments—that I am no longer anxious. As the Spirit told me on that fall day in the Kyoto Peace Garden in Holland Park, I am not going to be relieved of this "thorn in the flesh." But it can become strong, I have realized, when I refuse to use my anxiety as an excuse and instead exercise

some faith that the Lord can use my anxiety in productive ways. I have learned that the Lord is intimately aware of my struggles, even if He does not relieve me of them, just as He is aware of my hopes and triumphs. And this is a lesson that we should all learn. The Lord in fact needs me as His disciple—precisely because of my anxiety or other weaknesses as well as my strengths—just as He needs all of us. For those of us who suffer with anxiety, the burden of faith indeed at times seems heavy, but by being anxiously engaged, the Lord uses even that anxiety to bless others and, in the process, to lighten my own burdens. ✳

1.   Bruce C. Hafen, *A Disciple's Life: The Biography of Neal A. Maxwell* (Salt Lake City: Deseret Book, 2002), 16 (emphasis in original).

2.   Dietrich Bonhoeffer, *The Cost of Discipleship,* trans. R. H. Fuller, with some revision by Irmgard Booth (1937; repr. New York: Collier Books, 1963), 40.

James Rees

EXPANDING CIRCLES OF LOVE

What I Have Learned From Latter-day Saints

REV. DR. MARIAN EDMONDS-ALLEN

OST OF MY LIFE, I LOVED ALL people. That may sound disingenuous, but it's true. As a Christian, a follower of Jesus, it was important to me to try to love people as I thought God loved them—without noticing labels, without thinking about political affiliation or whether or not they shared my own type of faith. But for a time, I renounced all that because I thought there were some people, *those* people, who deserved to be hated. *Those* people, I am ashamed to admit now, were Latter-day Saints—the very people who ended up changing my life in ways I never expected. Isn't it so like God to turn something hurtful into a blessing beyond measure? Here is the surprising story of how Latter-day Saints changed my life.

In 2011, I was recruited to Salt Lake City to start a new LGBTQI+-affirming congregation for the United Church of Christ. I arrived just in time for the annual Utah Pride Festival, and the new church grew rapidly. We rented space in a charter school and immediately began an outreach for youth experiencing homelessness. We worshipped every Sunday and then cooked hot, nutritious meals that we delivered to sixty or so homeless youth in and around Salt Lake. These teens and children lived in camps, squats,

railroad cars, and empty buildings, hiding in plain sight. Utah was well known nationally at the time for rampant youth homelessness and, later, when we had the resources to track actual numbers, we found that five thousand young people—children as young as ten years old—experienced homelessness annually in Utah. About 42 percent of these young people identified as LGBTQI+, and about half had been kicked out of a religious home.[1]

These numbers don't even begin to hint at the lived reality of distress and loss that I encountered every day—teenagers and children who were discarded and kicked out of their homes (especially at major holidays, such as Christmas), young people who saw no future for themselves and sank into depression and suicidal ideation and completion. I became the executive director of an LGBTQI+ youth center in Ogden, and of the seven hundred youth who came through our doors every month, one-third were experiencing homelessness, and everyone knew someone who had died by suicide. One young person had lost nineteen friends to suicide.

Being new to Utah, I readily absorbed the attitudes of LGBTQI+ and allied circles at the time: the LDS Church was to blame; LDS members were to blame. In fact, religion itself was to blame.

> I continued my crusade against churches and Latter-day Saints, in particular, until I had my own Damascus Road moment—an experience that changed my life dramatically and forever.

And so, I left my parish ministry and became a crusader against religion, an activist who was increasingly angry. I was mostly angry that I couldn't find any help for these young people. But if I'm honest, I was also angry because my own tactics of shaming and blaming others weren't changing anything at all. In fact, things were getting worse. Because they were unaccompanied minors, these homeless LGBTQI+ youth and children were barred by state law from accessing shelters. That meant that sexual predators and human traffickers had a constant stream of children to target. Within thirty-six hours, almost every single young person experiencing homelessness would have some contact with a predator or trafficker, with results ranging from assault to being given drugs and waking in the back of a U-Haul trailer in a place far from their home.[2] Others died. There is a place above Salt Lake City called Suicide Rock, a tragic testament to what life for LGBTQI+ youth had become.

I continued my crusade against churches and Latter-day Saints, in particular, until I had my own Damascus Road moment—an experience that changed my life dramatically and forever. I met a Latter-day Saint, Laura, who I eventually realized cared as much about LGBTQI+ youth as I did. In the beginning, she was not an ally. Her traditional theology wasn't what we call "affirming" of LGBTQI+ people. I hated her at first, of course. But on the day my life changed, I saw that despite our differences of religion, politics, ideology—everything, really—her heart was a mirror of mine. After meeting a twelve-year-old LGBTQI+ boy who had been kicked out of his home, her heart changed. I could tell that she cared. She actually cared about LGBTQI+ young people. And not only did she care, she immediately went to work. She rallied her Relief Society friends to gather hundreds of coats for homeless youth. And then, because she was a Utah legislative aide, she got to work changing the law so that unaccompanied homeless youth could legally access homeless shelters in the state. Next, she went to work on suicide prevention and, after shepherding five laws through the Utah Legislature, she worked on creating a suicide prevention hotline that would help LGBTQI+ young people. I had told her that when young LGBTQI+ people called the existing hotline, they were often hung up on. So, she changed that—for Utah, and then for the entire country.[3]

God saw my hard, hateful heart and didn't give up on me. Instead, God sent someone to change my life. I know now that my calling from God is to tell my story and to encourage others to look for the surprising people who, though different from us, can join us in making a positive difference.

Many kind people thank me for my change of heart, but I don't deserve any thanks. Like the characters in some of the stories we read in the Bible, I wasn't interested in being loving. I was like Jonah, who fled from God's call. Jonah ended up in the belly of the whale before repenting and becoming a great prophet—or so the story goes. Saul of Tarsus persecuted and killed Christians before he was struck blind for a time on the road to Damascus. He repented and became the Apostle Paul, an inspiration to Christians all over the world, both then and now.

I'm not a hero like them. But I am someone that God decided to touch and teach a message that is now a gift for me to share with others. It is my calling from God to be honest with my own story, to be frank about the lessons and truths I have learned, and to be a human bridge for healing between frightened and hurting people.

One of the gifts God gave me that day on my own Damascus Road was an unshakable Christian faith and, along with that, a blessed release from the fear and hatred that had hardened my heart and shuttered my soul.

I learned how to stand strong in faith and to reach out with love. I learned that we need to free our hearts and our souls to shine with the love that has been given to us, to put our faith into action, to be strong in what we believe, and to reach out with courage to those who are different from us.

You will have to find your own way to do this, but for those who are interested in how I learned to stand strong in faith and reach out with love, here, in sum, are four simple truths I learned from my Latter-day Saint friends.

ONE: KNOW WHAT YOU BELIEVE

This may look different for you than for others. I have friends who are renowned religious scholars. They speak and write beautifully about scripture and theology. Their faith and beliefs fill books and sermons—gifts to all of us. Perhaps that is you! If so, thank you. Your scholarship is life giving. Jim, my advisor from years ago, is such a man. He is a New Testament scholar who shares insights and lessons that continue to inspire new thoughts in me and others.

Or perhaps you are like my friend Jan. One day she said to me, "Marian, I know I should be more interested in the theology of the church, but really, what is important to me is just following Jesus and knowing Him better." Jan puts her simple faith into action, helping people who are homeless, like she once was.

Is one way better than the other? I don't think so. The lesson for us is to simply know who we are, who God made us to be, and to understand our own faith.

TWO: BE COURAGEOUS

I learned the hard way that my fear was masked as hatred, and my hatred was killing the best parts of me. One of my favorite authors, Anne Lamott, writes in *Traveling Mercies*: "Not forgiving is like drinking rat poison and then waiting for the rat to die."[4]

I thought that my hard edges and sharp elbows kept me from the impurities of evil people. Instead, I was keeping the light of diversity from warming my soul. I needed these people I was holding at a distance. I need the world that God made, not the one I tried to make in my own image.

To accept that we need others and that we might be wrong about them requires genuine courage. We have to believe that our faith will only grow from being exposed to the faith of others. There is a warning sign I watch for every day: if someone's faith, belief, or perspective makes me defensive, I am not being courageous in my own faith.

One day, shortly after I'd moved to Utah, I met a man of faith, a prominent Latter-day Saint. I knew he was working in powerful ways behind the scenes to help LGBTQI+ people. I didn't understand why he would risk so much for someone like me who didn't share his religious beliefs when his religion isn't theologically affirming of my same-gender marriage. So, I asked him: "Why do you care, why do you do these things for me and people like me?" He reached out and took my

Elise Wehle

hand and looked into my eyes. Then he slowly said, with the hint of a shy smile: "It's my faith. It's because of my faith, you see."

Every day I try to have that courage.

THREE: SOLVE PROBLEMS

This man was working to solve a problem—the problem of the perceived competition between traditional Christian religious belief and LGBTQI+ dignity. He realized that, while he didn't believe in same-gender marriage, his belief in loving others meant that our conflicting beliefs could coexist in harmony.

There are two reasons why problem-solving is an important part of standing strong in our faith: (1) through working together to find harmony, we learn to appreciate each other's faith, beliefs, and perspectives, and (2) together, we are much more powerful and innovative than any of us can be on our own. Laura, for example, had ideas for solving the homeless youth problem that I'd never thought of. Laura didn't need to change her core beliefs—and neither did I. But working together, and with others, we found a solution.

FOUR: MAKE FRIENDS WHO ARE DIFFERENT FROM YOU

My LGBTQI+ friends often say: "I want to meet a Laura!" And my Latter-day Saint friends often say: "Why aren't there others like you?" The truth is, you already know Lauras and Marians, and others who are even more exceptional.

The key is letting your soul shine and then watching for those who enter into your expanding circle of light.

Listen to that voice in you, that prompting, that whisper (or maybe it's a loud shout!) that tells you to care. What you care most about, whether it's your church, our country, homeless youth, suicide prevention, strong families, education, the environment, democracy—whatever it is your soul longs for—that is your light, your calling, your superpower.

Look for others who share that same light, whoever they are, and get to know them—especially those who are surprising or have a different

> What you care most about, whether it's your church, our country, homeless youth, suicide prevention, strong families, education, the environment, democracy—whatever it is your soul longs for—that is your light, your calling, your superpower.

perspective and yet share your passion. Then find your harmony, the music that is uniquely yours and that, combined with the music of others, makes a pleasing sound—a sound our world needs.

You need to lean into your courage to do this. Don't be afraid. "Fear not!" is the most often repeated phrase in the Bible, occurring 365 times. This injunction reminds us that fear is the enemy of faith. When you reach out in love to someone surprising, notice any fear you may feel, and then smile at your courage. Listen to your soul, live your authentic faith without fear, lean into the moments you feel defensive, and let your heart shine with love.

Our world needs you—the real you, the courageous, faith-filled person of integrity that can love and work with others (even scary people like me; even scary people like you) to solve problems. We are all just people, beloved people at that. And our hearts and souls were made to shine! ✳

1. Marian Edmonds-Allen, Youth Pride Festival Survey Data Report (unpublished), Salt Lake City, UT, 2013.

2. Jay Olstad and Steve Eckert, "Homeless Teens Targeted by Sex Traffickers," Kare 11, November 5, 2015.

3. Marian L. Edmonds, "Covenant Pluralism, Religious Freedom, and Mission: Evidence for Healing the LGBT and Faith Divide" (doctor of ministry research project, Eden Theological Seminary, 2023), 64.

4. Anne Lamott, Traveling Mercies: Some Thoughts on Faith (New York: Pantheon, 1999), 134.

TO LIFE

KRISTEN
BLAIR

ON A RECENT WALK, MY THREE-YEAR-
old daughter and I came across a dead opossum
that had been killed by a car. My daughter was
fascinated by the animal's body and the drama
of its demise. For days, the "opossum story" was
told and retold. My daughter asked what had
happened. She asked about death and whether
all animals die. She asked if I will die. If she will
die. So we checked out books from the library. We
watched *Charlotte's Web*.

As the concept of death has become more
deeply entrenched in my little one's worldview,
I've noticed that her narrations about death often
involve the dead "coming back," usually echoing
the language we have supplied her from the
stories of Jesus's miracles raising the dead or his
own resurrection. Trained as a hospital chaplain,
I have noticed my desire to jump in and correct
her, to remind her that not all (not any) who die
come back. I've stumbled over language about
spirits and bodies and resurrection and heaven
and living again. Getting curious about my struggles with the topic, I've noticed my feelings of
resentment for these miracle stories which are so
out of tune with the human ordinary.

Jesus comes back. He breathes again, and
breathes life on his friends. The triumph of this
assertion is perhaps reliant on its uniqueness;
Jesus stands alone and apart, yet his very sep-
arateness bridges the chasms we feel between life
and death. Still I find myself believing more in
the cross, the tomb, and the grief of broken hopes
in the story's sequence. Maybe I find them more
relatable, these very human aspects of the narrative filled with flesh and blood and hunger and
pain. Maybe I struggle to find the same level of
resonance with the return, the coming back, the
reversing of finality.

Could we read the resurrection both as a story
of deity and *the* story of humanity? I am used to a
telling of this story that emphasizes overcoming,
triumph, and victory over the morbid forces of life.
But I wonder if this telling relies on paradigms

Jesus Mafa Series

that are not indigenous to the story. Easter Sunday does not erase Gethsemane, the cross, or the tomb. Easter Sunday, rather, emphasizes the constant return of life, and that this world is worth coming back to. Could renewal and return be, perhaps, the arc of the human Spirit, flowing indelibly with all of creation? Because death feels so very final, resurrection in turn feels distant. Especially for those who are bereaved, the cognitive belief in resurrection is almost never very comforting in the physical absence of a fleshy body. I look then not just to an abstract belief in a someday state, but to a story of renewal on a bright morning. To a reclaiming of what is human, even after the agony of a human existence. I look to a story of hope after hopelessness, and greeting after farewell. With such a lens, this may be the most human story of all: that life always perseveres, filling the vacuum of death. That the human Spirit is, above all, fiercely hungry for living, and that true death occurs only when that thirsty Spirit is finally quenched. Jesus's life and teachings did not center on asceticism or denial of life. Rather, they emphasized awakening. Internal turning and nourishment, transformed hearts, invigorated spirits, loving bodies: these are the radical teachings of Jesus, and the resurrection does not diminish them. Instead, the resurrection may be the ultimate moment of embodiment and with-ness. Life is worth returning to.

Jesus comes back to a body. To pain and suffering. To fatigue, hunger, desire. The resurrection might be read not just as an overcoming of mortality, but as a choice to be in solidarity with it. To claim it, love it, and uphold it.

To be alive is chaotic. No one is guaranteed protection from the fates of randomness and entropy and chance. Trying to control the future, or to refuse to hope for it, are tokens of the same coin of resistance to willing submission. To submit to life is to accept instability, to give up the idea that things happen for a divinely appointed reason. Instead, we create reason. We dig in the gardens of our lives and cultivate meaning. We bring ourselves to life as we progress toward death. We resurrect as we refuse cynicism and despair. We feed the Spirit that flows through all things and, by so doing, we live. Perhaps no phrase is better for the idea I am seeking than the Jewish *L'chaim*: to life!

There are both abundant paradoxes and abundant invitations to awe in this climax of the Jesus story. We return again and again, curious and wondering.

Full of life, my little one asks about death. I want to tell her the truth, and I want to shield her from the uncertainties I feel. And, with less anxious eyes, I see that the miraculous and the ordinary may not be such disparate things. Resurrection is all around us and constantly within us. The story of Jesus coming back is also the story of life bursting from ashes, and hope springing from long-closed hearts.

We are telling living stories, stories about ourselves and our world. We keep them alive in our bodies, tending to the cares of the day. It is enough. *L'chaim!* ❈

EMISSARIES

SUSAN
ELIZABETH
HOWE

An ungainly bird is the sandhill crane,
its spindly legs stretched like ropes
of silly putty, its pointy beak
of pointless length. Cinnamon chicks,
plain as their mother, scamper after
her ambitious wings, the dun blandness
of her feathers, the rouge-red smear
above her eyes, the white blotch below.
Soon they will grow as long as she,
have to bend almost in half to rough up
the undergrowth, to peck fallen corn
and beetles from fields, to ferret out frogs
in the shallows. Each chick sticks
with its mom, quaint and ugly.

But they are mythic creatures, perhaps
their bones remember. Eons ago,
two supernovae collided and blasted
them to Earth as particles,
no darkness the year of their arrival.
Certainly they have flown far
across the earth, a swoop to Siberia,
a swoop to the Shetlands.

Inside themselves, they must feel
a vibrancy more primordial
than beauty. You hear it in their staccato
harmonics, sound winding through
the long horns of their tracheas.
You see it in their dances,
bowing to honor each other,
then leaping, elated,
and on the way down, twirling.

EVERYTHING IS FULL OF GODS

A Review of Bettini's "In Praise of Polytheism"

CHARLES M. STANG

NCIENT ROMANS KEPT HOUSE-
hold shrines called *Lararia* (sg. *Lararium*).
Originally, they were meant to hold
statues of deities known as *Lares* (sg. *Lar*),
minor gods of uncertain origin, usually in pairs,
who protected the house and those who lived
in and around it, including livestock. Over time,
however, Romans would include in their *Lararia*
other gods, heroes, and even revered teachers.
The *Lararium* became, Maurizio Bettini tells us,
"something comparable to a private diary, in icono-
graphic form, of individual inclinations, emotions,
and experiences," that is, a shrine reflecting one's
personal, even idiosyncratic, spirituality. The
emperor Marcus Aurelius (AD 121–190) is said to
have included golden statues of his philosophical teachers in his *Lararium*. Another emperor,
Severus Alexander (AD 208–235), is said to have
included in his *Lararium* statues of deified emperors, portraits of his ancestors, and "holy souls,"
including Apollonius of Tyana, Christ, Abraham,
Orpheus, "and others of this same character."
What, we might wonder, are Jesus and Abraham
doing in the company of a pagan miracle worker
and a legendary Greek poet and prophet?

In his 2014 book, recently translated into
English as *In Praise of Polytheism*, Bettini

highlights how Alexander's *Lararium* exempli-
fies "polytheistic ways of thinking": "imagining
the gods with no hierarchy within a religious landscape able to bring together statues of ancestors, god-like emperors, philosophers, poets
and writers, heroes, saints, and moral guides"—
"even . . . figures from two different religious
systems." This is in stark contrast to monotheis-
tic thinking, exemplified for Bettini by Judaism
and Christianity (and later Islam). The irony is
that Alexander was tutored in Christian doctrine by none other than Origen of Alexandria
(AD 185–254), the Christian exegete and philosopher who was later condemned as a heretic in
an age of anxious orthodoxies. However broad-
minded Origen was, nothing in his writings
suggests that he would approve of Alexander
including Christ and Orpheus together in his
Lararium. Alexander, under the tutelage of his
mother and grandmother, seems to have been
something of a spiritual seeker. Unlike many of
his fellow emperors, he was tolerant of Jews and
Christians and is rumored to have prayed every
morning in a private chapel. But there is no evidence that he ever converted to Christianity.

Had he, it is unlikely that Alexander's *Lararium*
would have remained as it was, so capacious.

Ernst Steiner

That is because Christianity and Judaism are, as Bettini argues, exclusive monotheisms for which there is only one god (*monos theos*), and He alone is to be worshipped. And although Judaism and Christianity were the odd ones out in the ancient polytheistic Mediterranean world, exclusive monotheism eventually prevailed, thanks largely to Christianity's rise and the conversion of the Roman empire, and then to Islam's emergence and rapid spread. Bettini leans heavily on the work of Jan Assman, an influential if controversial Egyptologist and historian of religions. Assman frames Judaic monotheism as a "counter-religion": it understands itself not as one religion among many, but the one true religion awash in a sea of false faiths, which it must in some way or another oppose. Judaic monotheism had one significant ancestor: the pharaoh Akhenaten's failed attempt to establish an exclusive monotheism centered on the sun god Aten. But many centuries later, Moses, raised in Pharaoh's house, managed to succeed where Akhenaten had failed. The "Mosaic distinction," as Assman describes it, is a simple innovation: religion is now "true" or "false," and downstream of this distinction

are other familiar distinctions such as "Christian" versus "pagan," "Muslim" versus "infidel."

At the very center of Bettini's work is what he calls, following Williams James, the "cash-value" of polytheism. For James, "the cash-value of any concept . . . was in how the concept helped the individual to cope, how it aided the individual in his or her actual, practical and concrete experiences." What was the cash-value of polytheism, both in antiquity and today, such that Bettini wishes to sing in praise of it? He is clear that he favors "the specifically socio-political cash-value" of polytheism. In essence, Bettini argues, polytheism allows us to establish and navigate a relationship with other people's gods. It does so by way of translation and interpretation, and not by way of mere tolerance. Tolerance is the best card monotheism can play when facing the gods of others: since by the standards of monotheism those other gods are not real or true, they remain always a kind of fly in the ointment, an irritant that it might be impossible, or at least impolitic, to remove altogether. And therefore monotheism is caught between Scylla and Charybdis, either persecuting others into abandoning their gods, or begrudgingly tolerating these other gods and their worshippers.

Bettini thinks polytheism has more cards in its hand, including translation, not only between one language and another, but especially between one pantheon and another. He mentions translation charts from ancient Mesopotamia, correlating the gods of one language and culture (e.g., Sumeria) with those of another (e.g., Akkadia), including their respective spheres of influence. We're familiar with how the Greek gods were translated into their Roman counterparts: Zeus to Jupiter, Hera to Juno, Ares to Mars, Hephaestus to Vulcan, etc. The same was undertaken with the gods of Egypt, who hail from a more distant land, language, and culture. These efforts at translating one's own gods into the gods of others allowed for "a flexible attitude, spontaneously capable of creating integration and fusion, not separation, between different religious systems"; "a kind of common market of the gods."

The market metaphor continues as Bettini moves from one card to another, from translation to interpretation—which he insists on keeping in its Latin form, *interpretatio*, to remind us of the distance between the modern meaning of interpretation and the ancient. In Latin, the *interpres* is the person in a marketplace who stands between (*inter-*) two parties and sets the price

> There is much to praise about thinking in a plural fashion about the world around us, including the ancient polytheistic practices of translation and interpretation and the cultivation of curiosity.

(*-pres*) on whatever business is being conducted between them. Bettini writes: "In other words, the meaning of *interpretatio* is found within the sphere of negotiation and compromise. Consequently, giving an *interpretatio* of a specific utterance means specifically to propose a compromise, a mediation, between the utterance and its receiver." When it comes to interpreting one's own god in light of another's, one has to stand between both and—this is crucial—offer a *conjecture*, that is, a play or a pitch: might this mean that? Might this god of mine correspond to that god of yours, in *this* way, but perhaps not in *another* way? An interpretation is ventured; it is not certain. And so, it is always experimental, revisable, and open to debate: "this idea of the divine is in flux, I might say, and has its roots in the flexibility inherent to a polytheistic system, in its intrinsically open and creative nature."

Translation and interpretation in turn cultivate a distinct quality of mind, *curiosity*, which in Bettini's hands becomes the premier polytheistic virtue. He believes ancient polytheists were genuinely curious, interested in the gods of others and desirous to know them—both to know *about* them and to *know* them as persons and powers with whom they might profitably have dealings.

In contrast, he cites the acerbic early Christian apologist Tertullian: "We want no curious disputation [*curiositas*] after possessing Christ Jesus, no inquisition after enjoying the gospel. . . . Let such curiosity give place to faith. . . . To know nothing in opposition to the rule of faith, is to know all things."[2] For Tertullian, faith in Christ delivers certain knowledge of all things, and curiosity about anything that departs from that certain knowledge is a sinful distraction. Such certainty lends itself to violence. The Greeks and the Romans were each in their own way warrior cultures, as violent and bloodthirsty as any. But, Bettini insists, these polytheists never acted violently on specifically *religious* grounds: "this is such a striking, such an obvious fact that it usually ends up going unnoticed."

Throughout this book in praise of polytheism, Bettini reveals that he is more interested in "poly-" than in "theism." The "polytheistic ways of thinking" he praises amount to our "poly-thinking" about things, including gods:

> The plurality of gods did not constitute the essence of polytheistic religions as the name would make us believe, but merely the condition for bringing forth their most important virtue: *the capacity to think in a plural fashion about the world around them* and, at the same time, to provide equally plural methods for interpreting and intervening in this world. (my emphasis)

There is much to praise about thinking in a plural fashion about the world around us, including the ancient polytheistic practices of translation and interpretation and the cultivation of curiosity. But there is no real place in this paean for the gods themselves, *their* agency or agendas. There is no real place for the gods because, I suspect, for Bettini the gods are not real. This becomes especially evident in chapter 13, "Giving Citizenship to the Gods," which may be the most important and interesting of the whole book. If Roman polytheists were, as Bettini argues, curious about other people's gods, eager to translate and interpret them, how did they move from curiosity to official "recognition"? How did they admit new gods into the Roman fold? They did so by granting a new god Roman citizenship. The same verb—adscisco, "to recognize"—is used to make a human or a god a citizen. In a certain sense, it is only through becoming a citizen that a god can be said to be at all: "any given god 'was born' on the day of the public ceremony consecrating the temple and authorizing the god's entrance into the City."

It is we who make gods, not they who make us: "There is a fundamental principle behind all of these different examples, one that profoundly differentiates Roman religion from the one that substituted it: the conviction that the gods and their worship are a function of the human community, a consequence of them, and not the other way around." The substitute religion, of course, is Christianity, and Bettini is right that Christians do not accede to this order of things, humans making god(s). In his monumental City of God, Augustine excoriates this Roman idea that "divine things were instituted by men," but he preserves this quote from the Roman writer Varro in defense of it: "As the painter is before the painted tablet, the mason before the edifice, so states (civitates) are before those things which are instituted by states." For Romans, the state is the first principle, the axiom on which polytheistic postulates are built.

Bettini rather likes this Roman way of doing things. This method provides a check on any god, or his or her fanatical followers, who would try to enter the city unrecognized by the state. There is a certain "cash-value" of this Roman way for our contemporary lives, Bettini suggests. In Italy and elsewhere, we witness the fragmentation of identity according to ever more specific markers: where you were born, what dialect you speak, what food you eat. This becomes especially acute in the case of immigrants, who, because of the religion they practice (frequently Islam), are often not thought to be "fully" or "really" Italian, even if they are citizens. "Under these conditions," Bettini writes, "Italian society finds itself between a rock and a hard place: running the risk of breaking apart into many separate communities unable to communicate amongst themselves on one side; on the other, a reactionary form of forced cultural homogenization." He hopes that by elevating the status of the state and specifically citizenship, we can avoid either of these two poles. If citizenship is such a privilege that even the gods seek to have it, then perhaps it can once again become a concept with enough centripetal force to counter the centrifugal forces of both reactionary nativism and identity politics.

Despite its very interesting treatment of polytheistic ways of thinking—especially translation, interpretation, and curiosity—I confess I am left disappointed by this book in praise of polytheism precisely because it does not take theism seriously, which is to say it does not take the gods seriously. In Bettini's hands, the gods seem to be little more than the playthings of the state, and the coin of the realm is citizenship. Such a paean to (Roman) polytheism might appeal to a contemporary secular audience—just the sort of learned, post-Christian readers I imagine Bettini meant to address with his original publication in Italian in 2014—who, although they might read widely in communism, are, like good capitalists, only interested in the "cash-value" of anything ("what do we get from polytheism?"). But it does not appeal to this contemporary reader, who is increasingly tired of the Protagorean presumption that "man is the measure of all things." When will we allow that there are persons and powers beyond the human—some very familiar and close to hand, others more alien and harder to access—which we would do well to acknowledge and address? Perhaps no time soon, or at least no time soon in classical scholarship. If indeed Bettini is right and this is how the Romans thought of the gods—that we are the painters, and the gods our paintings (an ancient anticipation of Feuerbach); that they, like us, are seeking nothing more than citizenship—then I am inclined to look elsewhere than Rome, perhaps to Greece or to Egypt, for insights on how best to move in a world where, as the philosopher Thales of Miletus put it, "everything is full of gods." ✳

1. *Historia Augusta: Life of Alexander Severus*, trans. David Magie (Cambridge, MA: Loeb Classical Library, 1921), §29, 2.
2. Tertullian, *The Prescription Against Heretics*, trans. Peter Holmes, §§7 and 14.

WHAT ARE PEOPLE FOR?

Interview with L. Michael Sacasas

L. Michael Sacasas is the Executive Director of the Christian Study Center and author of the The Convivial Society, *a popular newsletter on technology, culture, and the moral life. Wayfare Editor Zachary Davis sat down with Michael to discuss the meaning of technology, why limits are good for us, and how to stay human in a dehumanizing age.*

How did you come to be interested in questions of technology?

The journey has a fairly straightforward starting point. While I was studying theology as a graduate student, I read sociologist Craig Gay's *Way of the Modern World*, whose premise is that many Christians tend to profess faith but live as if they were practical atheists. That is to say, their faith doesn't substantially impact the contours of their everyday life. In analyzing why that is, he examined the economic, political, cultural, and scientific technological structures that shape our habits and our assumptions in such a way that we end up living our lives counter to our expressed beliefs.

So the book caught my attention, and a particular chapter on science and technology introduced me to people like Lewis Mumford and

Hannah Arendt, to Martin Heidegger's work on technology, and to Jacques Ellul. And I began to think that technology is not just this thing we have around us that we use to accomplish banal, mundane tasks, or even to achieve great remarkable things like putting a man on the moon. Instead, technology is morally consequential, and its use has unnoted ramifications for how we seek to live our lives, for the kinds of communities we want to build.

At one point I began writing a blog called *The Frailest Thing*. I took that title from one of Pascal's *Pensées*. "Between us and heaven or hell there is only life, which is the frailest thing in the world." And I also published in *The New Atlantis* after the editor, Ari Schulman, reached out to me. *The New Atlantis* is such a wonderful publication that has shaped my own thinking for many years. The blog eventually became a newsletter, *The Convivial Society*. The newsletter isn't my day job, as I am currently the executive director of the Christian Study Center in Gainesville, Florida. It's a wonderful institution, loosely affiliated with about thirty to forty similar centers around the country. We try to cultivate a thoughtfulness informed by the Christian tradition about shared human questions, a regard for the intellectual resources within the Christian tradition, and to bear witness to that tradition in the university context.

I would say the root of my concern with technology is just simply a desire to know how we ought to live. What amounts to a good life and how does technology shape our ability to achieve, to some degree, the ideals we have for ourselves and for our communities?

The title of your newsletter is _The Convivial Society_. I love that word, _convivial_—it gestures towards relationality. In Mormon theology, the unit of salvation is a bit less individual than in Protestantism but extends to family and wider social relations. Joseph Smith, for example, was more city builder than single soul rescuer. He was forming a people and trying to build cities according to visions of utopia, of Zion. Could you talk a little bit about why you used the word _conviviality_ and the ways in which technology, the good life, and community interact?

Definitely. The word _conviviality_ is very closely linked, for me, to the work of Ivan Illich, a twentieth-century polymath. He was a historian and a social critic. In 1973, Illich wrote a book called _Tools for Conviviality_. I initially thought of my newsletter's title as a sort of homage to Illich's work, and then also to Jacques Ellul's _The Technological Society_. Both thinkers have been very important to me.

By the word _conviviality_ Illich was not talking about a bit of tipsiness at social gatherings; he used it specifically to oppose what he thought of as industrial society. It certainly has a communal dimension to it, and he was trying to describe and define the convivial society as an antidote or set of counter-practices to industrial society or a society shaped by industrial tools, by which he meant both technology and institutions, notably the school and the hospital, but also transportation, etc. Illich was trying to gather around that word—_conviviality_—an opposition to what he saw as the deficiencies and depredations of industrial society.

Convivial tools operate at a human scale, and so a convivial society is one that is conducive to

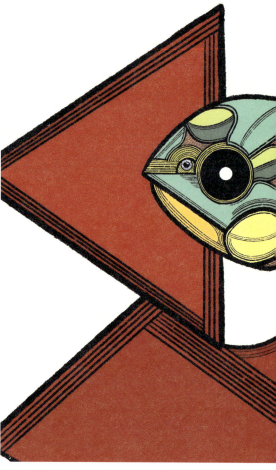

Joseph Chu

human flourishing on human terms. It operates at a scale and a pace that is hospitable to us as embodied human beings, that wouldn't dehumanize us by running counter to the conditions necessary for our flourishing. Conviviality entails both community and personal proficiency.

Illich saw that the industrial era was de skilling individuals. Industrial society makes individuals dependent on goods and services they cannot produce for themselves. And costs come with that, psychic costs, where we are unable to feel secure and competent in the world; social costs, where communities now outsource the fulfillment of needs to corporations or governmental services and agencies in ways that lift the burden of mutual care from the community to these industrial-scale institutions, where the individual gets lost and becomes a functionary, a number in a bureaucratic ledger.

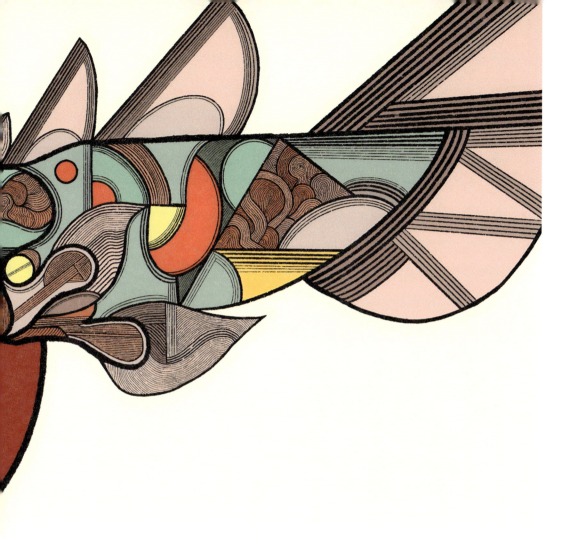

A convivial society, instead, has a sense of independence: a convivial tool is one that anyone could take up and learn how to use and master. To borrow Thoreau's term, the tool won't cause the user to become a tool of the tool. For Illich, that kind of autonomy and self-sufficiency always then served the community. We would have robust family units and small-scale communities and institutions in the service of interdependence. These would be the proper sites of human flourishing, sites that would empower individuals and users in their orbits rather than make them merely dependents of the services they would produce. Conviviality thus gathers much of Illich's thinking. It's not just a critique, but also a positive alternative vision for what has been lost and what ought to be cultivated.

I also think of conviviality as a spirit that one brings to life: seeking to build bridges, to be hospitable, and to welcome the stranger. Whenever he gathered with friends, Illich had this practice of lighting a candle that was supposed to symbolize, in one sense, the presence of the stranger who may come and join. In other words, we're always open to that surprise of a stranger's arrival. But in another sense, that stranger is also Christ, who is gathering with His people.

I think the very first difficulty of thinking differently about technology is defining what we mean by the word "technology." Before encountering your work, I probably would have defined technology as applied science or tools that help us achieve certain goals and, maybe more broadly, as symbols of progress. After your many years of reflection, could you share your own working definition of technology?

Joseph Chu

One of the things I found early on while writing publicly about technology was the difficulty of defining it well. And I'm afraid I don't end up with a very simple definition.

Typically, we think of words that are constructed like *technology—biology, geology, theology,* etc.—and we usually give them a standard definition, which is the study of whatever the prefix happens to be: biology is the study of life, geology the study of the earth, theology the study of God, and so on. The idea of "techn-ology" as a study of techne (Greek for "art" or "craft"), or the study of human making, that actually was the way in which the word *was* used, though rarely, as late as the nineteenth century. For example, when we think of the Massachusetts Institute of Technology, it's in that sense of "the study of techne" that the school was named in the mid-1800s.

But that doesn't quite work for *technology* in the way we commonly use it today. We use *technology* to refer not to the study of anything, but to an amazingly varied assortment of things. When I speak to groups on these topics, I'll look around whatever room I'm in and ask, "What is technology in this room?" For example, I'm holding a pen and I'm writing on a piece of paper, both of which count as technologies. We tend to think of it first as our tools. But when we push beyond the question of tools, when we ask how did this pen and paper get to me, then we imagine a whole machinery behind the mass production of pens, the creation of ink, the manufacturing of paper. We think of the industry that turns trees into stuff we hold in our hands.

In that sense *technology* becomes a very unhelpful term: it includes too much, and by doing so it veils. It becomes impossible to ask, Are you pro-technology or anti-technology? The question is senseless. You can't make it mean anything because it is impossible to declare yourself either for or against technology without reservation.

So what we need to do is look at specific technologies and systems at a more granular level. We need to examine how they operate and what they require of us, what they allow us to do, how they change our relationships with our communities, and what kind of self they generate when we're thinking about our engagement with media technology through which we express ourselves and receive information about the world. From there emerge all sorts of questions we can then ask. But *technology,* that word itself, often gets us into trouble or leads us down the wrong path.

Consider the railroad. We could just look at it as a technological artifact. But of course it's composed of countless other parts, and it would be inadequate to stop there. The railroad car could not function unless a system of tracks were created. That rail system then necessitated not just further artifacts but a systemization of society. We created time zones in order to make train travel coordinated and safe. Time zones then systematize the human experience of time in the United States. Social consequences! Consider also the automobile and its effects in creating urban and suburban communities, all of the social ramifications resulting from the systems necessary to sustain the given artifacts. Throughout the nineteenth century, these systems became more elaborate and more complex.

It's that line from Heidegger: "The essence of technology is by no means anything technological." If you're just looking at the tools, the artifacts, or even the systems, you end up missing that there's also a way of looking at the world through the lens of the technological. You see the world as a space of problems to be solved through the application of technical means. An example that drove this home for me several years ago was Noah Yuval Harari talking about a trend in the way we think about death. This universal human experience that has been the subject of such profound moral, cultural, artistic, and theological reflection, that has been central to the human understanding of what it means to be a human being across cultures, simply gets reduced to an engineering problem. According to that view, if we just begin to look at death as an engineering problem, we may solve it. That's a radically different way of experiencing and intersecting with the world around us.

When you continue to dig and ask questions regarding the moral ramifications of technology, you end up inevitably coming to this question of what are people for, which is a question from Wendell Berry. Only when you ask that question

We are embodied creatures, and one of the theological pillars I bring to my thinking about technology is that the body is good and its limitations are good.

do you have a position from which to think critically about technology. What are people for? What is the good life? What is the just society? And then think about how technology abets or hampers our pursuit of the responses to those questions.

Berry has a wonderful line in one of his Sabbath poems, that we live the given life and not the planned. It's the idea of receiving the world and creation as a gift. That is in jeopardy when we begin to adopt a technological way of thinking about the world. The world then becomes a field for mastery, for the application of our will. And we lose sight of it as a gift that, at least to some degree, ought to be received with gratitude.

Heidegger, famously, had the idea of thrownness, so distinct from the idea of creation as a gift. Thrownness is so violent, you're just tossed down on this rock, and the trauma immediately puts you into a scarcity mindset where you have to think about how to compete and survive. Whereas your view (and Berry's) is that it's a gift to come down and be conscious and receive these wonders to explore. It's a very different framing.

Right, exactly. Receiving the world with gratitude is an important aspect of that way of being in the world. It doesn't mean that we can't act in the world or on the world, but that we bring a different set of values into our relationship with the world and one another. We may see it less as a matter of manipulating the world towards our own ends and more a matter of also receiving and caring and learning from the world around us. That's a long way of talking about what technology is. But we have to consider every one of those levels of how technology becomes a part of our lives, how it interacts with our own aspirations of who we want to be.

One of the most popular things you have written was a set of forty-one questions that people can ask themselves about the technologies that they're using. You wanted to show that whether technology is good or bad depends on a number of factors, including how you interact with it.

Many Americans, religious people especially, feel extremely anxious about technology. Ideas and patterns and invitations can come through smartphones that seem to present harm to the community, to people's children or partners. Though this isn't new, there's heightened anxiety about the role of the internet, and many don't feel in control.

These questions are very helpful because they remind you that you are in control or that you at least have more control than you think you do. But who can ask forty-one questions of themselves every time they try a different device? So rather than necessarily going through all forty-one questions, what is the pattern of thought or heuristic that you're trying to encourage people to use as they encounter these new things in the world?

The first thing the questions all presume is that technologies are not neutral. We have not thought more deeply about technology in part because we have assumed that technology is inherently neutral and what matters is what we do with it. In other words, the use to which humans put technology is where all the moral value rests. Our second assumption is that technology as a whole is a largely beneficent force in human history. So the questions first seek to disrupt those assumptions.

One way of thinking about this first idea—that technology is not neutral—is the old expression that to the person with a hammer, everything looks like a nail. That expression neatly captures a kind of phenomenological approach to technology: when a tool comes into the circuit of mind, body, and world, it changes our perception of the world. This is not to suggest that anybody who takes a hammer is going to go around hitting everything around them. It can be more subtle. But it does suggest that your intentions are

directed in some way when you take that tool in hand. To use the hammer, you recognize that even its shape, its weightedness on one end, the way it fits in your hand—it encourages you to see everything around you as something that you could hit, even if you're not necessarily going to hit it.

Consider what happened when we began carrying cameras around with us all the time: every interaction, everything you see, every walk you take, the world subtly shifts, and all of these things become things that could be photographed and documented, regardless of what we're seeing or doing. Then link that shift in perspective to Instagram or Facebook. It changes the character of our experience. Even if you never take the picture, as you're walking you may think, "Oh, that would be a nice shot to post on Instagram." You didn't do a bad thing or a good thing. You may not even have done anything at all with the tool. But the tool itself, its presence—its way of mediating our experience which is going to raise questions, present possibilities, some might say create temptations.

The underlying heuristic of the questions is simply to become thoughtful. To recognize that when we pick up these tools, in one way or another, they're shaping our experience of the world, our relationships, and our self. You can look at those questions as iterating the same questions for those three groups: self, community, and nature or creation or the world. We should think about how the tool affects us at those three levels. You don't have to learn the 41 questions. I could have written 141 questions. The point was simply to generate thoughtfulness towards the tools. Whatever insights I may have had about technology, I derived most of them simply by paying attention to myself, by being very introspective about how a certain tool was working on me, how it was shaping me, what compulsions it might be creating in me, how it encouraged me to act or not to act. If we take the time to think reflectively about our own experience, we may find that we can all be pretty good tech critics in the sense that we become attuned to the ways in which these technologies in general shape our lives and the character of our relationships, and so forth.

I would mention one other thing, and that is

Joseph Chu

that the body has become a very important point of analysis. We are embodied creatures, and one of the theological pillars I bring to my thinking about technology is that the body is good and its limitations are good. If we think about how technologies may encourage us to disregard the body, to be thoughtless about the body, maybe to even hold the body in scorn, or how technology may displace the body as a focal point of human experience—we begin to think about that circuit of self, community, world, and how, when you interject the tool into that circuit, it begins to shape the working of the whole.

I want to hear more about how your theological or religious commitments have influenced your thinking about these questions. It seems to me that perhaps the most important theological inheritance from Christianity that can inform current debates is the incarnation: that the material world and our material bodies are good and worthy and should not be seen as problems to escape or to re-engineer.

When I consider the theologically informed principles that form the foundation of my thinking, I think of the *goodness* of creation. That has

ramifications for how we think of ourselves as human beings and for how we relate to nature. Theologically, we would speak of nature as creation. What is our responsibility or obligation towards the created world?

Modernity has given us a pretty strict separation between the human and the non-human. But theologically I see us as part of a created order, distinct in some ways but also as members of a community that includes not just humans, but the land and other creatures and elements that share the world. We must think about how technology impacts our relationship to the created world. In doing so, we must remember creation's fundamental goodness. And a key part of that goodness is its embodiedness.

Whether I think of the declaration of the goodness of the embodied human being at creation in Genesis or the incarnation or the resurrection of the body—these key doctrines that inform the Christian understanding—they all affirm the value of the embodied human condition. And as you put it, that it is not something we should seek to re-engineer or to escape.

So often in the story of technology in the modern West, even from the outset, there was this desire to alleviate the human estate. Francis Bacon puts in terms of ameliorating the effects of the Fall. But that very quickly changed to a goal of transcending the human condition. In my view, we should instead recognize that the limits entailed in our humanity don't necessarily exist to be transcended, but that they're conducive to our flourishing. We should think about the idea that creation is gratuitous, that it is a gift, and what that means for how we relate to the world, how the tools we use encourage us to receive the world as a gift, or discourage that posture. Different ramifications spill out from there.

A lot of angst about smartphones, for example, stems from what I think of as distraction discourse or attention discourse. That discourse focuses on the negative, this sense that we're losing our capacity to focus. But the discourse rarely gives place to the goods towards which our attention ought to be directed. Part of a religious perspective is to have a clear sense of what those goods are and why we ought to be, at least

One of the most difficult things Jesus has commanded us is to turn the other cheek; that runs very much counter to the grain. But perhaps more difficult in these times is His command to take no thought for tomorrow, that we lay aside the imperative to control and to manage and to fine-tune every aspect of our lives and bring it all within our control.

in some ways, curbing our use of technology. Not because we're anxious or reactionary, but because we want to pursue a certain set of goods. When tools impede that pursuit, we should recognize that those tools ought to be relegated to their proper place so that we can free ourselves to pursue those goods.

Hope also plays an important part in this. Theologically, our hope is ultimately not in our own resources. That keeps certain theologically informed technology thinkers from giving ourselves up to the idea that that technology will be our savior, that if we just find the right technological fix then things are all going to be well.

You said one thing that I think goes against deep American optimism, which is that limits can help us flourish. Christians in general believe in adhering to God's law, not because God merely wants us to be obedient or because He loves to exert control, but because those laws ultimately lead to a greater freedom in a more abundant life. Is that what you have in mind when you see limits as being conducive to our ultimate joy?

Part of the image that comes to mind when I think about this is a passage in an essay by Wendell Berry, "Faustian Economics (Hell hath no limits)." He has a wonderful, very articulate paragraph in which he talks about how a small plot of land, when cared for, can actually yield indefinitely. It has this capacity to be continuously renewed and to give its fruit. On the one hand there's this sense that I don't just need more and more and more to live the good life; the good life is not just a matter of endless accumulation. Instead, it recognizes that limited things, or limited scale, cared for and attended to properly can be rewarding and can be a source of satisfaction and joy. It goes against the grain of a decidedly consumerist American culture. Indeed, if the ways we are shaped by our consumer technologies have an overall pattern, it is simply to cultivate in us the presumption that the good life is the life that one can purchase or consume. Instead of this ideal of endless consumption, we can recognize a better path to joy and happiness, and a sense of satisfaction and purpose in this life. Law, certainly in a sense of moral prohibition, is properly understood as a way of channeling us towards the good rather than simply arbitrary limitations.

One other way in which limits go against the grain of some strains of American culture is in recognition of our obligation to one another, our interdependence. For example, the choice to stay in a community to care for your aging parents instead of moving to an exciting new city. That could be a case where you might embrace the limits of your obligations to your family and consume less exciting resources and opportunities. But those very limits may also point towards a greater fulfillment or a greater sense of one's harmony with life itself. At its best, religion is a school of love. One of my favorite things about Latter-day Saint life, and one relatively unique to us I think, is that you can't really choose which congregation you go to. You go to the one in your geographic area. You can't shop around to find one that's a closer match to your preferred race or income or political affiliation, which means you have to learn to love people

that you would otherwise not choose to. In this way, we find that through the limiting of our choices, we grow into beings that we most aspire to be.

That's an excellent example.

As a final question, do you find any other resources within the Christian tradition or within the story of Jesus that might inform how we can have a healthier relationship to the human-built world or that could help us deepen our relationship with God and one another?

There could be many answers to that question, but the one that comes readily to mind is how parents think about technology in their children's lives—I encourage readers and listeners not to think primarily about limitations but to think about the virtues that they want to aspire to, something to focus on. This is not just a matter of being positive. There is some good whose beauty is drawing us toward itself and that we value, that we long for. And because we want to pursue that good, we want to mitigate the ways in which we might be hampered from pursuing it.

The life of Christ provides us with an example to be followed.

Lately I have been reflecting on Jesus's lack of hurry in the gospels. It's striking. In fact, at the one point where He is being pushed to hurry, when His friend Lazarus is ill, He decidedly refuses to hurry in a way that frustrates all of those around Him.

I think about the frenetic pace of our lives, about the way in which we always feel ourselves fighting for time (or just fighting time), not even able to abide moments of stillness. We should reflect deeply upon what is giving shape to the temporal structures of our lives such that we are kept from modeling the example of Christ in this very specific way. There is the felt experience of time when we are with those who need our care, who need our attention. One of the costs of the perpetual state of hurriedness, the frenetic standstill, is that we may find ourselves impatient with our children, impatient with our neighbors, impatient with those that need something of us, impatient maybe even with ourselves. We should think about how we might better structure our lives, including the tools we use to structure that experience, so that we might better approximate being at peace with time.

One of the most difficult things Jesus has commanded us is to turn the other cheek; that runs very much counter to the grain. But perhaps more difficult in these times is His command to take no thought for tomorrow, that we lay aside the imperative to control and to manage and to fine-tune every aspect of our lives and bring it all within our control. We have many tools to do that, to manage and control and master our experience in the future rather than creating an openness, a hopeful openness to surprise. Indeed, Illich's term for grace is an openness to the surprise that may come, and a lack of anxiety. The more we are bent on controlling, the more anxious we become. That calmness of spirit that Christ models for us is also a product of a complete dependence upon the Father's good gifts. That disposition runs very much counter to how our technological infrastructure is marketed to us as tools to control the world and bring about what we want in it.

Joseph Chu

GAINING THE KNOWLEDGE THAT SAVES

NATURE OF SAVING KNOWLEDGE

No Salvation in Ignorance of Gospel. There never was a time, I suppose, in the history of the world when so much knowledge was in the possession of men. Surely knowledge has been increased, but at the same time, the doctrine taught in this prophetic saying by Paul is true: men are ever learning, but apparently never able

LUSTERWARE

Crafting a Genuine Spiritual Life

LAUREL THATCHER ULRICH

I HAVE BEEN THINKING LATELY about an Emily Dickinson poem I first heard twenty-five years ago in an American literature class at the University of Utah. I remember feeling intrigued and somewhat troubled as the professor read the poem since he was reported to be a lapsed Mormon. "Was that how it felt to lose faith?" I thought.

> It dropped so low—in my Regard—
> I heard it hit the Ground—
> And go to pieces on the Stones
> At bottom of my Mind—
> Yet blamed the Fate that flung it—less
> Than I denounced Myself,
> For entertaining Plated Wares
> Upon my Silver Shelf.—

Since then I have lost faith in many things, among them Olympia typewriters, *New York Times* book reviews, and texturized vegetable protein; and yes, like most Latter-day Saints, I have had to reconsider some of my deepest religious beliefs. I have always been a somewhat skeptical person. I can remember raising my arm in Beehive class in the Sugar City Ward and telling my teacher that regardless of what she said I did *not* think that polygamy was sent by God. That kind of behavior may have had something to do with the palm reading I received from another teacher at an MIA gypsy party. She traced the lines on my upturned hand and told me my "head" line was longer and better developed than my "heart" line. For a while I worried about that.

As I have grown older, I have become less fearful of those "stones at the bottom of my mind." In fact, I am convinced that a willingness to admit disbelief is often essential to spiritual growth. All of us meet challenges to our faith—persons who fail to measure up, doctrines that refuse to settle comfortably into our minds, books that contain troubling ideas or disorienting information. The temptation is strong to "blame the fate that flung it" or to ignore the crash as it hits the ground, pretending that nothing has changed. Neither technique is very useful. Though a few people seem to have been blessed with foam rubber rather than stones at the bottom of their minds (may they rest in peace), sooner or later most of us are forced to confront our shattered beliefs.

I find Emily Dickinson's little poem helpful. Some things fall off the shelf because they did not belong there in the first place; they were "Plated Wares" rather than genuine silver. At first I didn't fully grasp the image. The only "Plated Wares" I knew anything about were made by Oneida or Wm. Rogers. Although less valuable than sterling, that sort of silverplate hardly falls to pieces when dropped. Then I learned about lusterware, the most popular "Plated Wares" of Emily Dickinson's time. In the late eighteenth century, British manufacturers developed a technique for decorating ceramic ware with a gold or platinum film. In one variety, a platinum luster was applied to the entire surface of the object to produce what contemporaries called "poor man's silver." Shiny, inexpensive, and easy to get, it was also fragile, as breakable as any other piece of pottery or china. Only a gullible or very inexperienced person would mistake it for true silver.

All of us have lusterware as well as silver on that shelf we keep at the top of our minds. A lusterware Joseph Smith, for instance, is unfailingly young, handsome, and spiritually radiant; unschooled but never superstitious, persecuted but never vengeful, human but never mistaken. A lusterware image fulfills our need for an ideal without demanding a great deal from us. There are lusterware missions and marriages, lusterware friendships, lusterware histories, and yes, lusterware visions of ourselves. Most of these

Charlotte Condie

will be tested at some point on the stones at the bottom of our minds.

A number of years ago I read a letter from a young woman who had recently discovered some lusterware on her own shelf. "I used to think of the Church as one hundred percent true," she wrote. "But now I realize it is probably *ten percent* human and only ninety percent divine." I gasped, wanting to write back immediately, "If you find any earthly institution that is ten percent divine, embrace it with all your heart!" Actually ten percent is probably too high an estimate. Jesus spoke of grains of salt and bits of leaven, and He told His disciples that "the kingdom of heaven is like unto treasure hid in a field; the which when a man hath found, he hideth, and for joy thereof goeth and selleth all that he hath, and buyeth that field" (Matthew 13:44). Thus a small speck of divinity—the salt in the earth, the leaven in the lump of dough, the treasure hidden in the field—gives value and life to the whole. Now the question is where in the Church of Jesus Christ of Latter-day Saints do we go to find the leaven? To the bishop? To the prophet? To the lesson manuals? Do we find it in Relief Society? In sacrament meeting? And if we fail to discover it in any of these places shall we declare the lump worthless? Jesus' answer was clear. The leaven must be found in one's own heart or not at all: ". . . the kingdom of God is within you" (Luke 17:21).

Many years ago a blunt bishop countered one of my earnest complaints with a statement I have never forgotten: "The Church is a good place to practice the Christian virtues of forgiveness, mercy, and love unfeigned." That was a revelation to me. The Church was not a place that exemplified Christian virtues so much as a place that required them. I suppose I had always thought of it as a nice cushion, a source of warmth and comfort if ever things got tough (which they seldom had in my life). It hadn't occurred to me that the Church could *make* things tough.

Eliza R. Snow expressed it this way in a hymn that seems to be missing from the new book:

Think not when you gather to Zion,
Your troubles and trials are through,
That nothing but comfort and pleasure

Are waiting in Zion for you:
No, no, 'tis designed as a furnace,
All substance, all textures to try,
To burn all the "wood, hay, and stubble,"
The gold from the dross purify.

Probably the hymn deserved to be dropped from the book. The third stanza suggests that the author, like more than one Relief Society president since, had made too many welfare visits and had listened to too many sad stories. Her charity failing, she told the complainers in her ward to shape up and solve their own problems:

Think not when you gather to Zion,
The Saints here have nothing to do
But to look to your personal welfare,
And always be comforting you.

In the Church, as in our own families, we have the worst and the best of times.

A young missionary on a lonely bus ride somewhere in Bolivia thinks he is equal to what lies ahead. He can endure hard work, strange food, and a confusing dialect. But nothing in the Mission Training Center has prepared him for the filthiness of the apartment, for the cynicism of his first companion, or for the parakeet who lives, with all its droppings, under the other man's bed.

A young bride, ready to enter the temple, feels herself spiritually prepared. By choosing a simple white gown useable later as a temple dress she has already shown her preference for religious commitment over fantasy. She has discussed the covenants with her stake president and she feels she understands them. Yet sitting in the endowment room in ritual clothing no one had thought to show her, saying words she does not understand, she turns to her mother in dismay. "Am I supposed to enjoy this?" she says.

An elders quorum president, pleased that his firm has won the contract for the ward remodeling project, prepares for the hard work ahead. He knows the job will be demanding. He expects some tension between his responsibilities as project manager and his commitment to the Church, but he is ready to consecrate his time and talents for the upbuilding of the Kingdom.

As I have grown older, I have become less fearful of those "stones at the bottom of my mind." In fact, I am convinced that a willingness to admit disbelief is often essential to spiritual growth.

What he doesn't expect is the anger and the humiliation that follow his year-long encounter with the Church bureaucracy. "I wonder how far up this sort of thing goes?" he asks, and contemplates leaving the Church.

A middle-aged woman reads deeply in the scriptures, sharing her insights with friends individually and in a small study group. She feels secure in her quest for greater light and truth until she begins to examine certain troubling episodes in Church history. The discrepancy between the official accounts and the new accounts distresses her. Has she been lied to? And if in one issue, why not many? Confiding her doubts to her friends, she feels them back away.

"And the rain descended, and the floods came, and the winds blew, and beat upon that house; and it fell not: for it was founded upon a rock" (Matthew 7:24–25). What rock can secure us against such storms? Occasionally some gentle soul, perhaps as puzzled as my Beehive teacher by my outspoken ways, will ask, "What keeps you in the Church?" "My skepticism," I answer, only half in jest. Over the years I have noticed that Saints with doubts often outlast "true believers." But of course the answer is inadequate. I don't stay in the Church because of what I don't know, but because of what I do.

The Church I believe in is not an ascending hierarchy of the holy. It is millions of ordinary people calling one another "brother" and "sister" and trying to make it true. Not so long ago I had one of those terrible-wonderful experiences that I have been talking about. It started in an innocuous way, then built to a genuine crisis—a classic Liahona–Iron Rod conflict between me and my bishop. After a week of sleepless nights I went into his office feeling threatened and fragile. What followed was an astonishingly open and healing discussion, a small miracle. As I told a friend later, "If we hadn't been Mormons, we would have embraced!" Our opinions didn't change much; our attitudes toward one another did. I give him credit for having the humility to listen, and I give myself credit for trusting him enough to say what I really felt. The leaven in our lump was a common reaching for the Spirit.

I am not always comfortable in my ward. There are weeks when I wonder if I can sit through another Relief Society lesson delivered straight from the manual or endure another meandering discussion in Gospel Doctrine class. Yet there are also moments when, surprised by my own silence, I am able to hear what a speaker only half says. Several months ago, as I was bracing myself for a fast and testimony meeting, a member of the bishopric approached me and asked if I would give the closing prayer. I said, "Yes," feeling like a hypocrite, yet at the same time silently accepting some responsibility for the success of the meeting. Were the testimonies really better? When I stood to pray I was moved to the point of tears.

For me the issue is not whether the Church of Jesus Christ of Latter-day Saints is the One True Church Upon the Face of the Earth. That sounds to me like a particularly Zoramite brand of lusterware:

> Now the place was called by them Rameumptom, which, being interpreted, is the holy stand. Now, from this stand they did offer up, every man, the self-same prayer. . . . We thank thee, O God, for we are a chosen people unto thee, while others shall perish. (Alma 31:22, 28)

The really crucial issue for me is that the Spirit of Christ is alive in the Church, and that it continues to touch and redeem the lives of the individual members. The young man survived his mission, returning with a stronger, more sober sense of what it meant to serve. The bride returned to the temple and enjoyed it more. The elders quorum

president, though still struggling with his anger, knows it is his problem to face and to solve. The middle-aged woman grew through her loss of faith into a richer, deeper spirituality.

As I study the scriptures very few contemporary problems seem new. I wonder how men in tune with the divine can appear to be so complacent and self-righteous in their dealings with women. Then I read Luke's account of the visit of the angel to the women at the tomb on the first day of the week: "It was Mary Magdalene, and Joanna, and Mary the mother of James, and other women that were with them, which told these things unto the apostles. And their words seemed to them as idle tales, and they believed them not" (Luke 24:10–11). I wonder how a church purportedly devoted to eternal values can invest so much energy in issues that strike me as unimportant. Then I read the nineteenth chapter of Leviticus and find the second greatest commandment, "thou shalt love thy neighbor as thyself," side by side with a sober command that "neither shall a garment mingled of linen and woolen come upon thee" (Leviticus 19:18–19). Every dispensation has had its silver and its lusterware. God speaks to His children, as Moroni taught us, in our own language, and in our own narrow and culture-bound condition.

To me that is a cause for joy rather than cynicism. I love Joseph Smith's ecstatic recital in Doctrine and Covenants 128:

> Now, what do we hear in the gospel which we have received? A voice of gladness! a voice of mercy from heaven; and a voice of truth out of the earth. . . .
> A voice of the Lord in the wilderness of Fayette, Seneca county. . . .
> The voice of Michael on the banks of the Susquehanna. . . .
> The voice of Peter, James, and John in the wilderness between Harmony, Susquehanna county, and Colesville, Broome county. . . .
> And again, the voice of God in the chamber of old Father Whitmer, in Fayette, Seneca county, and at sundry times, and in divers

Charlotte Condie

places through all the travels and tribulations of this Church of Jesus Christ of Latter-day Saints! (D&C 128:19–21)

Joseph's litany of homely place names, his insistence that the voice of God could indeed be heard on the banks of an ordinary American river or in the chamber of a common farmer, gives his message an audacity and a power that cannot be ignored. For me Joseph Smith's witness that the divine can strike through the immediate is more important than any of the particulars enshrined in the church he established. If other people want to reduce D&C 128 to a data processing program for handling family group sheets, that's fine. I am far more interested in that "whole and complete and perfect union, and welding together of dispensations" that Joseph wrote about.

Two or three years ago I attended a small unofficial women's conference in Nauvoo. The ostensible purpose was to celebrate the founding of the Relief Society, but the real agenda was to come to terms with the position of women in the contemporary Church. The participants came from many places: a few of us known to each other, many of us strangers, the only common bond being some connection with the three organizers, all of whom remained maddeningly opaque as to their motives. I cannot describe what happened to me during those three days. Let me just say that after emptying myself of any hope for peace and change in the Church I heard the voice of

the Lord on the banks of the Mississippi River. It was a voice of gladness, telling me that the gospel had indeed been restored. It was a voice of truth, assuring me that my concerns were just, that much was still amiss in the Church. It was a voice of mercy, giving me the courage to continue my uneasy dialogue between doubt and faith. I am not talking here about a literal voice, but about an infusion of the Spirit—a kind of Pentecost that for a moment dissolved the boundaries between heaven and earth and between present and past. I felt as though I were reexperiencing the events the early Saints had described.

I am not a mystical person. In ordinary decisions in my family I am far more likely to call for a vote than a prayer, and when other people proclaim their "spiritual experiences" I am generally cautious. But I would gladly sift through a great trough of meal for even a little bit of that leaven.

The temptations of skepticism are real. Sweeping up the lusterware, we sometimes forget to polish and cherish the silver, not knowing that the power of discernment is one of the gifts of the Spirit and that the ability to discover counterfeit wares also gives us the power to recognize the genuine. ✽

This essay previously appeared in A Thoughtful Faith: Essays on Belief by Mormon Scholars, *ed. Philip L. Barlow (Centerville, UT: Canon Press, 1986), 195–204. A shorter version first appeared as Laurel Thatcher Ulrich, "Lusterware,"* Exponent II 11, *no. 3 (Spring 1985): 6.*

WRITERS

BRINN ELIZABETH BAGLEY is a poet and nature-based educator living in a farmhouse in rural Idaho with her daughters, husband, a herd of bison, and nine cats.

JEANINE BEE is the fiction editor for *Wayfare* and a Pushcart Prize–nominated writer. Her writing has been featured in places such as *Exponent II*, *Irreantum*, and *Dialogue*. She lives in Utah with her husband and four kids.

STAN BENFELL is the director of the David M. Kennedy Center for International Studies and professor of comparative literature at Brigham Young University.

KRISTEN BLAIR works with practical theology and lives in Toronto, Ontario.

MATTHEW BOWMAN is Howard W. Hunter Chair of Mormon Studies at Claremont Graduate University and the author of *The Mormon People: The Making of an American Faith* and *The Abduction of Betty and Barney Hill: Alien Encounters and the Fragmentation of America*.

ALIXA BROBBEY is a student at Brigham Young University and has written for *Dialogue: A Journal of Mormon Thought*, *Exponent II*, and the *Mormon Lit Blitz*, and she was recently selected as one of six winning artists for the Artists Residency at the Center for Latter-day Saint Arts.

AUGUST BURTON is pursuing his bachelor's and master's degree in Biomedical Data Science from Stanford University. He plays excessive amounts of pickleball, derives great pleasure from wearing shirt-jackets, and is a major proponent of the Oxford comma.

LIZ BUSBY is a writer and scholar currently doing graduate work at BYU on intersection between Mormonism and science fiction/fantasy. Her writing has been published in BYU *Studies*, *Irreantum*, and SFRA *Review*.

STEPHEN CARTER is the director of publications at the Sunstone Education Foundation and author of *Virginia Sorensen: Pioneering Mormon Author*. He is the recipient of the 2023 Smith-Pettit Award for Outstanding Contribution to Mormon Letters.

ZACHARY DAVIS is the Executive Director of Faith Matters and the Editor of *Wayfare*.

REV. DR. MARIAN EDMONDS-ALLEN'S call from God is to be a healer of divides. She is the executive director of Parity and the author of *Covenantal Pluralism*, *Religious Freedom and Mission: Evidence for Healing the* LGBT *and Faith Divide*.

JAMES EGAN works as an attorney in health care in Salt Lake City, Utah. He is the treasurer of Mormon Scholars in the Humanities, and his most recent release of piano-led pop rock is the album *Invisible Light*.

TERRYL GIVENS is Senior Research Fellow at the Maxwell Institute and author and coauthor of many books, including *Wrestling the Angel* and *The God Who Weeps*.

JAMES GOLDBERG is a poet, playwright, essayist, novelist, documentary filmmaker, scholar, and translator who specializes in Mormon literature.

KRISTINE HAGLUND is a past editor of *Dialogue* and the author of *Eugene England: A Mormon Liberal*.

GRANT HARDY is a professor of History and Religious Studies at the University of North Carolina at Asheville.

AMY HARRIS is an associate professor of history and family history/genealogy at Brigham Young University. Her research interests center on families, women, and gender in early modern Britain.

LIZZIE HEISELT is a reader, writer, runner, and mother living in Brooklyn, New York. She studied American Studies at BYU and Journalism at NYU.

LAURA REECE HOGAN is the author of *Butterfly Nebula* (Backwaters, University of Nebraska Press, 2023); winner of the Backwaters Prize in Poetry, *Litany of Flights* (Paraclete Press, 2020); winner of the Paraclete Poetry Prize, the chapbook *O Garden-Dweller* (Finishing Line Press); and the nonfiction spiritual theology book *I Live, No Longer I* (Wipf & Stock).

SUSAN ELIZABETH HOWE is the author of the poetry collections *Salt* (2013) and *Stone Spirits* (1997), which won the Charles Redd Center Publication Prize and the Association for Mormon Letters Award in Poetry.

LOGAN MICKEL is an English instructor at Weber State University, where he teaches courses on writing, rhetoric, and superheroes. His work can be seen at AsMuchGood.com.

JOHN DURHAM PETERS teaches and writes on media history and philosophy. He is the María Rosa Menocal Professor of English and of Film & Media Studies at Yale University.

JOHN ROSENBERG is a retired BYU professor of Spanish and American Relations.

L. MICHAEL SACASAS is the Executive Director of the Christian Study Center of Gainesville and the author of *The Convivial Society*, a newsletter about technology, culture, and moral life.

KATHRYN KNIGHT SONNTAG is the Poetry Editor for *Wayfare* and the author of *The Mother Tree: Discovering the Love and Wisdom of Our Divine Mother* and *The Tree at the Center*.

JOSEPH SPENCER is a philosopher and an assistant professor of ancient scripture at Brigham Young University.

CHARLES M. STANG is Professor of Early Christian Thought and Director of the Center for the Study of World Religions at Harvard Divinity School.

ROBBIE TAGGART is a teacher and poet who delights in the holiness of the everyday.

LAUREL THATCHER ULRICH is 300th Anniversary University Professor *emerita* at Harvard University, a cofounder of *Exponent II*, and the author of *A Midwife's Tale: The Life of Martha Ballard Based on Her Diary, 1785–1812*, which won the Pulitzer Prize for History.

CANDICE WENDT is a writer who supports students of all backgrounds and belief systems in their spiritual lives at McGill University's Office of Religious and Spiritual Life.

ETHAN F. WICKMAN is Professor of Music Composition and Theory at the University of Texas at San Antonio.

CHARLOTTE WILSON is an editor and writer running a small business between school pickups. She lives with her family in the Pacific Northwest, loves watching shows late at night with her husband, and ignores the laundry piles in favor of a good book.

STEVE YOUNG is a two-time NFL MVP, now president and cofounder of HGGC, a private equity firm, and founder of the Forever Young Foundation, a global charity for children, which he cochairs with his wife, Barb. He lives with his family in the San Francisco Bay area.

ARTISTS

Daniel Mitsui

TYPESET IN JOSHUA DARDEN'S FREIGHT TEXT   AND HOEFLER & COMPANY'S SURVEYOR AND DECIMAL

PRINTED ON 60LB TEXT PAPER   21 MAR 2024

PRINTED AT NORTH STAR PRINTING, SPANISH FORK, UTAH